God
Who Are You?

David Huyard

2009

PRESS

Dedicated in Honor of our Children

Grandchildren & Great Grandchildren
&
Our Future Generations

May the Lord's favor be with them to continue
and complete
Through them what we were unable to
accomplish for His glory.

Melvin & Ann
Grandson Eric & Tanya
Great Grandchild Shea

Rose & Lou
Grandsons, Michael & Colin

Dale

Dwight & Susan
Grandchildren, Leah, Isaac, Luke, Benjamin

Crystal
Grandchild Kendra

Contents

Forward
By

Kerry Willis, Vision Pastor
First Church of the Nazarene

Davison Huyard is a seeker "after" God's heart. The very title of the book you are reading validates it-GOD WHO ARE YOU? If we do not want to know Who God Is, then we are living our earthly lives in the opposite direction of Eternal Hope.

GOD WHO ARE YOU? Is in part the chronicle of a young Amish boy who began early to seek a personal relationship with the God of Heaven and Earth. Surrendered to the Spirit of Truth, the boy, David, literally left the cornfields of his childhood to be God's man on the Mission Fields of the world. Why? That he may know God intimately and that he might make God known to others.

David writes as he lives-passionately. My prayer is that as you read this book, you will see beautiful colors added to the canvas of your earthly life-eternal colors that only Heaven can create. May you come to passionately know Who God Is, for who He truly is-the one called Wonderful!

Preface

"**G**od who are you!" Every person is confronted with this question in one way or another, from the most remote jungle regions of the world to the elitist of society, people want to know who the true God is, but more than that, the true believer wants to experience God. Who He is and how He desires to relate to our individual lives is the question each person has to answer for themselves with a personal faith in what He has provided for our salvation in the finished work of the cross.

No one will ever know who God is without the discovery of God's One and only Son, Jesus Christ, who became God in the flesh to reveal to humanity the Father. As creator of all life forms, Jesus Christ is the only one who could create His own mother and in God's time be conceived in her womb by the Holy Spirit, the creator of the universe becoming Mary's biological child with God as His Father, to become Mary's Savior and to birth out of Himself a universal eternal spiritual family.

The title of my book is simply meant to be thought provoking, challenging the reader to discover a greater dimension of God through His Son Jesus Christ, by the indwelling presence and power of the Holy Spirit and then to commit one's life to the Lordship of Christ at any cost, to discover a greater dimension of who God is by reading God's Word, the Bible, and becoming conformed to that Word living a consistent Christian life.

For years Anna Mary and I recorded words that were aired on the airwaves around the world, many of those words found a lodging place in some person's heart, for the most part they cannot be recalled and only eternity will reveal the harvest that will come out of the seeds that were sown using words, we believe, that the printed page will outlast our lifetime and for this reason we desire to tell our story in this way.

God spoke everything into being by the Word of His power, out of His Spirit; words are the most powerful force coming out of our spirit. Words can hurt or heal, condemn, or redeem, and can be both negative and positive; negative words are difficult to forget; even God who is all power cannot recall our ill-spoken words. The only way to deal with unkind, harsh, negative words is to forgive and forget.

The Holy Spirit will always help our heart to forget what our mind wants to remember.

We all know what it feels like to be rejected, but we should never accept rejection. Rejection will never perform its hurtful work in our lives if we refuse to accept it. Jesus Christ was rejected so that we might live with an attitude and spirit of acceptance to find spiritual and emotional healing over the works of the enemy.

Our positive words spoken into the atmosphere by faith will always move mountains, including obstacles and obstructions placed before us. When we pray, the atmosphere is shaken as our words ascend to God's throne as incense becoming a sweet smelling savor. God will always honor our prayers in the name of Jesus.

By praying in faith that God, who is able, with a child-like trust, we can call things into being that are not as if they already were; a spiritual dynamic comes into place when we intercede with supplication and thanksgiving. To intercede simply implies we are standing in the gap for the other person, by our supplication, we are reminding God of His promise to us by our humble, earnest entreaty, and to always be thankful for His mercy and grace which He renews every morning of each new day with a baptism of His love for us as individuals and the world which He loves.

With the Holy Spirit in our lives, we cannot lose, we can only win. We might at times be hindered, but we will not be defeated. We may at times not know what to say, but we will not be silenced. We have a faith that is determined to allow the Holy Spirit to produce life in us that is established deep in the River of Life, therefore, we become as a river flowing and bearing fruit. When our faith is fundamental and established in the Word, the fruit that comes forth from our lives will be holy, as well as appealing and acceptable to the beholder.

We are God's people in the world today to win the world to Christ. Not only are we as a voice crying in the wilderness living our lives among sinful humanity; we are His voice in the market place, or wherever our presence is felt. We have delegated authority as extensions of Jesus to speak for Him in His name.

God called us forth, birthed out of Himself for this time in history to be His people, as a holy nation, and a royal priesthood of believers as a witness of who He is. We have heavens' full attention and assistance with an army of angelic hosts going before us to make us more than conquerors.

God's people have always lived in days of uncertainty, but in spite of that we experience a mighty deliverance, *"the weapons of our warfare are not carnal but mighty to pulling down strongholds,"* we will always have our spiritual weapons to engage in battle with a target to pursue and to conquer in His name.

When we allow the Holy Spirit to reconstruct our thinking by transforming our mind, we can always think deeper thoughts, and live on a higher standard of life. If we only live by what some other person said, then all we will ever know is what someone else has said, and we will never discover the power of what God has already spoken and what He still wants to speak into our individual lives. His Words are Spirit and Life and, *"...God magnifies His Word above His name,"* (Psalm 138:2). God's Word will still stand after the present heaven and earth have passed away.

Our birth certificate establishes the record of who we are and the lineage from where we came; we are expressed revelations out of God, created in His image for this time in history to build the Kingdom of Christ so that future generations might know the Lord.

Our genes will establish the chronological lineage of who we are while we live, and of whom we were following our demise. The challenge of our prayer life is to realize that we must not only pray for our generation now, but that our lineage continues on by the lives that will come forth out of our loins long after we leave this world. These people will decide by their lives the state of their spirituality and the rise and fall of their generations by the way they serve the Lord.

Time and history records God's masterpiece of events and people and how they chose to serve Him, we are responsible before God to invest our prayers into our future generations, this is why we as parents and grandparents must realize we have prayer power to shape future generations that will also reap a harvest of souls for God's Kingdom.

God will birth generations out of us to complete what we had desired to accomplish, including missionaries, doctors, nurses, preachers and teachers, only eternity will reveal the final impact of our life lived on earth.

When Jesus taught the disciples to pray, *"Your Kingdom come on earth as in heaven,"* this is exactly what He had in mind; we will never understand the entire scope of God's desired intent until we realize we can shape the future by our intercessory prayer life.

Only as we download God's software into the hard drive of our heart will we be able to retrieve His promised Word to us to be faithful in our devotion and service, our lives coming to full fruition for His glory.

Our desire is that as you read our story and accept our admonition into your spirit, you will be challenged to a greater determination to be a conqueror in Jesus' name, by living your life to the full as the Holy Spirit brings completion to your life on the earth with a legacy of faith that will impact future generations, that you will purpose in your heart to live in God's will and prepare to make heaven your eternal dwelling place, "see you there!"

- Dave

Chapter One

God Please Help Me!

The heart-cry of the universe has been reaching the heart of God ever since the dawn of creation and through the century's mankind has been on a continual search to know their creator God. Even a child wants to know who God is. The faith of a child meant so much to Jesus that He said, *"...assuredly I say to you, whoever does not receive the Kingdom of God as a little child will by no means enter it,"* (Mark 10:15).

Only as we humble ourselves before God will we be able to breakthrough into His realm to experience God as our Abba Father, having a Father Child relationship.

Who in the world is more humble and dependent on their parent than a little child? Those who come to God must always come to Him with a child-like dependent faith, the measure of our faith always determines the strength of our assurance which reflects the extent of our commitment to Christ, and no one will ever experience God's peace without completely resigning to His LORDSHIP. God has placed more value on one individual soul than the total worth of the world and invites us to come to Him and make Jesus Christ Lord of our lives.

Jesus welcomed the little children to sit on His lap to illustrate how we all have to come to Him; just as we are, so He can make us as He is, that is to be made righteous by His life with a full complete dependence upon Him for our entire well being.

No matter what our station in life is, our rank and file or level of intelligence and achievements, we all have to come to God the same way; that is, to His cross to discover who He is, to confess Jesus as Lord and repent from our sins and by faith receive Him into our heart.

Allow your faith journey to be a challenge as you discover peace and identity with God, and to know what it means to be a born-again Christian. I found great fulfillment in the vision God gave me as a child, and the many revelations of His continued will as I lived my life day by day. Our prayer is that your journey of faith might also cause you to be more than a conqueror over the things that you struggle with, and to become drawn into a greater knowledge of what the Lord still wants to do with our lives together for His glory.

As a child I wanted to know who God is more than anything in life. This search and my quest for knowledge would take me on a long journey of discovery. It would mean leaving everything that I knew that was dear to me to follow Jesus Christ into the greatest adventure anyone could hope for, with the greatest fulfillment in so many areas; including learning about other cultures, to become one with the many Christians that I would meet, an on-going circle of friend-ships, to break bread with them as they invited me into their lives, their homes and their churches, visiting many coun-tries of the world including the islands of the sea.

This journey would involve the exploration of my gifted-ness in ministry, including the fascinating world of art and music, and to work by helping other people discover those hidden talents and gifts that lay dormant in their lives, but most of all, my desire is to share how I pursued the high calling of God to proclaim the gospel of Jesus Christ which would take me from the cornfield of an Amish farm in Lancaster County, Pennsylvania to the mission fields of the world via international radio broadcasting, including crusade and pulpit ministry and the public market place winning souls for the Kingdom of Christ.

My greatest discovery would come as I personally accepted Jesus Christ as my Savior, to become a born again Christian, to be baptized with the power and anointing of the Holy Spirit upon me to preserve and deliver me through discouraging and dangerous situations, to rescue me from the sin and failures of my life to pursue my calling.

Still today my greatest satisfaction and soul-joy happens as I see individuals break through in victory over their sin and struggles to surrender their lives to Christ, making Jesus Lord of their lives.

There are as many descriptions and interpretations of who God is as there are stars in the sky. Prophets have proclaimed and described Him from the beginning of time, and through the centuries. God has provided humankind with revelations of Himself in many ways; but not until the Holy Spirit of God indwells an individual can we have any concept or spirit life within us, and when this happens the Holy Spirit will take us into the depth of God with an understanding of who He desires to be in us and how He wants to perform revelations of Himself through us to the world as light shining in a dark place. This is the only way that we can become the person we were designed to be and the only effective way to help anyone no matter how great their problems are.

Revelations concerning my life would happen as I refused to be defeated by events or circumstances; I was a child that had no idea of who God was other than He was the good man in heaven and we were taught to respect Him, and if we lived good lives we would hopefully go to heaven when we died.

A magnetic drawing power within me became a spiritual force that would not let go of me. An awareness of the presence of the Holy Spirit in me increased with every obstacle and defeat that I encountered. This would become the story of my life. From the valleys of discouragement and disappointments, through seasons of defeat, sin and failure only to be restored, refreshed and forgiven, and always taking me to a higher purpose of commitment with a deeper level of relationship in Jesus Christ, up and down, but always going through in victory, from extreme ecstasy to be drawn into the realm of the Spirit as I felt the freedom and the anointing that comes by soaring as an eagle, to those days when I would rather die than live.

Only as I discovered my life in Christ did I better understand who God is and that Jesus Christ had become man in the flesh to identify with our humanness and our sin, and to reveal to humanity the love that God has for the world. God is sinner friendly not willing that anyone person should perish without knowing Him through His Son Jesus Christ, and to experience the forgiveness of sins and the assurance of everlasting life in Christ.

Finding God is an Adventure

God has a sovereign will and unique purpose for every person born into the world and has provided people with an instinct to search for Him with all of their heart so strong, that no demon power can withstand us with the promise that if we seek for Him we will discover who He is.

The greatest tragedy for any person would be to miss knowing God as their heavenly Father, and Jesus Christ as personal Savior with the indwelling presence and power of the Holy Spirit to inspire and guide them through life. Yet millions go to their graves never discovering or to experience this awesome relationship. I happen to be one of those fortunate individuals born into a rich heritage of faith and life. I could have been born into a heathen family to never experience what has become the greatest adventure any person could desire.

My Amish heritage has carried me through many difficult situations that otherwise could have defeated me; we were taught to work hard and endure hardship. To work at achieving our goals in life, to live separated lives from the world, to respect our fellowman, including our government, and to be our brothers' keeper, but above all, to respect and honor our creator God.

Known as a quiet or silent people of the land, the Amish have a powerful silent witness that has touched and influenced the world in many ways. As any other people group, there are those who have a greater knowledge and commitment to the Lordship of Christ knowing what it means to be born from above.

I could have found fulfillment and enjoyed my life on the farm my parents had purchased for me. Something of God takes shape within our being by living close to the earth. Just to experience the harshness of winter, we anticipated springtime to walk behind the plow all day long, day after day, tilling the soil with the smell of the earth, to plant seeds and to watch that crop emerge from the ground to again reap a bountiful harvest.

To harvest the wheat and watch the small grains emerge out of the old fashioned threshing machine powered by a steam engine, neighbor helping neighbor, being depended upon each other realizing that apart from our neighbors we could not sustain life and prosper.

The vision I had in the cornfield of preaching to thousands of black people would have never become real had it not been for other people the Lord brought into my life. I would have taken that unfulfilled assignment with me to my grave. Now that I'm an older man, to reflect is to rejoice, to be able to say with the apostle Paul, I too have fought a good fight and I have kept the faith; however, my course is not yet finished since I still have a ministry to complete with many more discoveries of who God is and how He wants me to complete my assignment before He calls me into His presence.

The same dynamic principles that worked so well on the farm would apply on the mission field as well, together with friends and partners; we would plow new ground and sow seed for the Lord working together as a team to harvest souls for Jesus. Much of the tools to make this happen were also primitive, but they worked because God revealed Himself in the harvest.

Our discovery of God involves our search for who He is and how we were designed by Him to relate to Him. Our desperation to know Him through an intimate relationship determines the depth of His revelation to us; we were all born to serve the Lord and there is a powerful dynamic taking place within our heart even though unrealized by many individuals. Before we even think about pursuing God, He has already been pursuing us before we were born and His promise to us is — He will not leave us nor will He forsake us.

God has set His people as a seal upon His heart, His love for us is stronger than death, this was confirmed to Isaiah when God told him that He would *"...inscribe our name in the palm of His hand,"* (Isaiah 49:16).

Jesus reiterated this promise concerning our identity with God by saying, *"I will never leave you nor forsake you, and no one will pluck you out of My Fathers hand."*

God Has Spoken, it is Written

God has already answered the question, God who are you? The entire Bible is a revelation of God including His

Son Jesus Christ and His Holy Spirit. God sent His one and only Son into the world to reveal the Father to humanity and after Jesus returned to the Father, He sent the Holy Spirit to convict the world of sin, judgment and righteousness, and to also be our daily guide and counselor while we live in this world. Jesus said,

> *"I have come that you might have life, and have it more abundantly,"*

(John 10:10).

The apostle Paul said,

> *"The mystery which has been hidden from ages and from generations, but now has been revealed to His saints. To them God willed to make known what are the riches of the glory of this mystery among the Gentiles; which is Christ in you, the hope of glory,"*

(Colossians 1:26-27).

Old Testament saints walked and talked with God leaving a rich heritage of faith as an example for us to follow. By their commitment they changed the course of history. We have an advantage over them since they could not pray with delegated authority in the name of Jesus neither did they experience the indwelling presence and power of the Holy Spirit. As their story was recorded, so is ours, and we too are changing the course of history in our day, every time we win a soul to Jesus we not only change the course of human lives and history, we impact eternity for the glory of God.

No one has stooped so low in sin but God will pardon and forgive. Jesus came to prove that by His death on a cross and by His resurrection power over death providing us with new life, eternal life, to pick us up where He found us to wash and cleanse us with His redeeming blood to experience the forgiveness of sins, becoming tools in His hands to plow the fertile soil of the world producing a rich harvest of souls for His Kingdom.

God as in the past is speaking to His world today with a powerful redemptive voice; He does this in diversified ways, through His church and the many outreach ministries of world evangelism, but most effectively as we become a spiritual significant other in someone's life as one beggar telling another beggar where they found bread.

> *"God who at various times and in various ways spoke in times past to the fathers by the prophets, has in these last days spoken to us by His Son, whom He has appointed heir of all things, through whom also He made the worlds; who being the brightness of His glory and the express image of His person, and upholding all things by the Word of His power, when He had by Himself purged our sins, sat down at the right hand of the Majesty on high, having become so much better than the angels, as He has by inheritance obtained a more excellent name than they,"*

(Hebrews 1:1-4).

As a child, God always seemed remote to me, so very far away; there was nothing personal about Him that I could relate to, I could not feel Him inside of my lonely emptiness even though I longed for Him with all of my heart, my understanding of the new birth was a complete mystery; even though my inner desire was to experience anything to satisfy the longings of my heart. If you struggle with this issue then keep on reading and allow my testimony to encourage you to trust the Lord with your life and soul, He will bring the greatest fulfillment into any one persons' life no matter who they are or what they did. God desires to bring the greatest meaning and purpose into our lives that the things of this world could never accomplish.

Gazing out the window watching the cloud formations from the small Amish country school where I attended distracted me from my studies. God who are you, where did you come from? I had to know. That would all change when years later I experienced the Holy Spirit transforming my heart and providing me with a purpose and a driving force within me determined to live my life for Jesus Christ, but I had to search for Him with all of my heart and still do since He reveals only so much of Himself as we progress in our faith walk with Him. There are days we feel as if He is hiding His face from us only to appear before us with unexpected revelations and blessings of Himself as we mature and progress in our faith life in Him.

As with every individual, the Holy Spirit is in the world today, *"to convict the world of sin, judgment and righteousness,"* the nations of the world and every individual are without excuse if they fail to discover Him. We are invited to knock at His door but before we become aware of our need to do that He has already been knocking at our door. God wants us to have a fellowship relationship with Him in this life, to spend eternity together with Him to discover who He really is when our eyes will behold Him face to face, when the fullness of our life's assignment is complete, and the fullness of His glory will be revealed to us in Christ and the beauty of heaven He prepared for us becomes real.

Untold millions of individuals have left this world with unfulfilled aspirations as they felt God calling them into service. God provided them with glimpses and even revelations of Himself, but the obstacles were too great and their faith and trust too small; they gave in to defeat to live unfulfilled lives and so they died.

Adam had the greatest call that God had ever placed upon a human being. God revealed Himself to Adam through the creation process. Adam was created from the ground, "humus or dirt,", God breathed into Adam the breath of life, and Adam became a living soul to experience God as no other human being ever did, Adam was created in the image and likeness of God living in the glory of God's presence without sin yet given the privilege of making moral choices.

Adam experienced what no other human being ever experienced; that was to look His creator in the face, eye to eye, and together in the garden God and Adam celebrated life in the perfection of Gods creation. Adam and Eve had an untarnished perfect relationship with God until they yielded to temptation, together they died a spiritual death and that death sentence passed upon all humanity and now we also stand guilty before God until we accept His provision for our redemption and sanctification. We, too, stand before God untarnished as a result of what the second Adam, Jesus Christ has provided for us on the cross by His own blood which makes us righteous before God and, "Free indeed!" through the perfection of Christ. Now God's face has become veiled until that day when in our glorified bodies we will see Him face to face.

The serpent was now sentenced to crawl on the very ground from which God had created man to never be able to experience the freedom that the second Adam would provide by redeeming the souls of man living in a forgiven relationship.

All mankind as Adam also made wrong choices, we all have felt the consequences of those choices and many of us have paid a great price and in many ways with great regret for our sin, since God is not willing that any person perish without experiencing His forgiving grace. He invites us to come to Him to be forgiven and set free, anytime or place, and in any situation or condition.

Before we can know God as our heavenly Father, it becomes our responsibility to seek God for ourselves; no one else can do that for us. This discovery can happen anywhere, in a large gathering of people, or when we are all alone. And unless the Holy Spirit is present to transact the transformation nothing spiritual happens and when transformation takes place no individual or demon from hell can distract or stop the work of redemption. To reject the provision God made for our redemption has indescribable eternal consequences. To accept Jesus Christ as our personal Savior there are eternal blessings beyond our comprehension.

"Eye has not seen, nor ear heard, nor have entered into the heart of man the things which God has prepared for those who love Him,"

(1Corinthians 2:9).

My desire to know God intensified as I grew older and not until He revealed Himself to me in a personal way did I realize that He wants to have a personal relationship with me and that He had a special assignment for me that would provide me with a greater understanding of who He is and of who I was meant to become.

Growing up as a small Amish boy, I had limited knowledge about God. I still do, since His ways are past finding out, but I have discovered God as my heavenly Father, my "Abba Daddy" my personal friend which has become an intimate growing process of exploring who He is through the revelation of His Word and by the experiences He brings into my life, but most of all by the power of the Holy Spirit who lives inside of me and the conversations we have with each other.

No one can discover God for us. People can assist, encourage, instruct, mentor and pray for us. However, to receive God's Holy Spirit into our heart is a personal choice every individual has to make for themselves; God can be known as we seek for Him with all our heart.

> *"Seek the Lord while He may be found, call upon Him while He is near. Let the wicked forsake his way and the unrighteous man his thoughts, let him return to the Lord, and He will have mercy on him; and to our God, for He will abundantly pardon,"*

(Isaiah 55:6-7).

God always extends an open invitation for any individual to come and discover who He is, it was a long process involving time and patience until the promised Savior of the world was introduced by John the Baptist. Four thousand years of history evolved with many types and shadows pointing towards the coming redeemer who would reveal the Father and redeem a sinful humanity.

The death and resurrection of Jesus Christ opened up a new and living way to come to the heart of God. It takes some individuals a life-time to discover this and surrender to the Lordship of Christ and become born-again Christians. However, to procrastinate is to gamble with our eternity. To not search for truth is to choose to remain ignorant and suffer the consequences, to simply not care is arrogance toward God and one's own eternity, to die a lost soul is a great eternal tragedy.

God has placed more value on one individual soul than the worth of the world. He paid a great price to purchase our soul by offering up His One and only Son to die for our sins, the least anyone can do is accept Him as Savior and Lord, living a life of obedience by following Him in true discipleship and thereby reaping the blessings and benefits of His favor upon our lives.

God's Kingdom is within the Believer

Pentecost, the coming of the Holy Spirit would provide the believer with new understandings and revelations as the Holy Spirit opened the Word of God to the believer. The entire Bible reveals God's revelation of love for the world of humanity which He created; the Bible begins with a revelation of the coming Savior and His Kingdom which is to come, the pre-flood prophets proclaimed the Kingdom of God and every time an individual receives Jesus Christ as their personal Savior the Kingdom of God comes to this earth and will yet come into its full fruition when Jesus reigns on the earth as King of Kings and Lord of Lords according to, (Revelation 19:11-16).

"Come" is the greatest invitation in the entire Bible, providing a continual invitation to learn to know God for who He is and to grow in His grace, the invitation to come and accept Christ extends for *"whosoever will may come,"* from Genesis to Revelation.

Jesus said.

> *"Behold I stand at the door and knock. If anyone hears my voice and opens the door, I will come in to him and dine with him and he with Me. To him who overcomes I will grant to sit with Me on My throne, as I also overcame and sat down with My Father on His throne,"*

> (Revelation 3:20-21).

God could not close the curtain on time as we know it without one more invitation to come into a personal relationship, and before He comes, to rapture His Bride the Church, and before He creates the new earth and the new

29

heaven following His thousand year reign on the earth. He instructed John to extend one more on-going invitation to accept His love through Jesus Christ until that day when the Holy Spirit and the Bride of Christ leave this present world. The Holy Spirit, who indwells the bride of Christ, the church, is making an all-out effort to invite the lost to come and receive Christ and be saved before it is too late.

"And the Spirit and the bride say, "Come!" And let him who hears say, "Come!" And let him who thirsts come, whosoever desires, let him take the water of life freely,"

(Revelation 22:17).

On the Great Judgment Day men and nations will be without excuse, mankind has been created by God who breathed within man His breath and who sustains mankind by His power, science has tried to analyze and explain God, religion has tried to describe Him many times for that which He is not, to reject Him for who He is. Philosophers have tried to explain Him by their practical wisdom, atheists have tried to deny His existence, but sincere seekers have discovered Him as the pearl of great price, the Savior and salvation of their soul.

Revelations of God are every where; He is seen in the conception of all life forms and the birthing of all creation, even a still born child has God's resurrection power within them to also come forth on the resurrection. God has revealed Himself through the physical universe being able to count and name every star; He has revealed Himself through His Word, and above all through His Son Jesus Christ and by the power of the Holy Spirit who indwells His people as His witnesses upon the earth.

"The heavens declare the glory of God; and the firmament shows His handiwork. Day unto day utters speech and night unto night reveals knowledge. There is no speech nor language where their voice is not heard. Their line has gone out through all the earth and their words to the end of the world"

(Psalm 19:1).

In John's gospel Jesus is revealed as the Word of God, *"... that in Him all things were made through Him, and without Him nothing was made that was made. In Him was life, and the life was the light of men,"*

(John 1:1-4).

Since Jesus Christ is the creator of all life forms, He would be the only God-man that could create His own mother, and to also become her only Savior, and out of Himself by His Spirit created a universal spiritual family of God.

Chapter Two

Unveiling the Mystery

The mystery of God is unveiled in the revelation of His Word. Jesus Christ came to earth to reveal to mankind the Father, and Jesus is the only door into God's Kingdom.

Everything that God created is a revelation of Himself as the Creator. He introduced Himself in the Garden of Eden as in no other way when He fashioned Adam in His own image and likeness, breathing into Adam the breath of life and man became a living soul.

The entire human race came forth out of Adam as God's creation with a soul that will never die, providing us with a body to become indwelt by His Holy Spirit so that we might live eternally with Him and purposed by His will that we should become an extension of who He is in our world today as a witness for Christ and His Kingdom. God's greatest revelation, however, comes to us from the inspired written record, the Bible, as the Holy Spirit reveals to us God's One and only Son, Jesus Christ.

To unveil the mystery of who God is has engaged men and nations on a quest of discovery from the beginning of time, digging through the archives of history and the earth itself, scanning the universe to either declare Him or deny

Him, even trying to place God under a microscope only to discover He is much too vast and His ways past finding out.

For centuries individuals have discovered meaning and purpose through a personal relationship with God. This is why He simplified that process by sending His One and only Son into the world to reveal to humanity who He is and when we discover the reality of Jesus Christ, and the power of the Holy Spirit in us, we will discover the reality of God which will embark us on the greatest adventure of a lifetime.

Jesus said,

> *"I am the way, the truth and the life. No one comes to the Father except through me. If you had known Me, you would have known My Father also, and from now on you know Him and have seen Him.*

> (John 14:6-7).

God has always provided those moments of opportunity for every individual to discover Him in a personal relationship, even though our finite minds limit us to a full and complete understanding of the infinity of God. Since God has created every person individually unique, there are no two people who will experience the same encounter, even though they are similar in nature and always for the same purpose; that is to redeem us from our sinful nature re-creating us through the new birth process and to make us aware of His call upon our lives as a witness of His grace; this was the purpose of Christ's mission to this earth.

God's desire and design for us is to be supreme over us as our heavenly Father, to also provide us with everything we need to excel in life as in death, since in Him we shall never die. Our spirit in life as redeemed, longs to be joined to our glorified body following our resurrection, in the meantime, we live as His royal subjects upon the earth, giving Him praise and glory by the way we live our lives before Him in this world, including the testimony and legacy of faith we leave following our demise.

Our personal discovery of God and our response to that discovery may never be quite the same with diversified revelations, commitments and assignments, but always for the same purpose; to bring honor and glory to Him by the way we serve Him as Lord of our life. For some people this means serving Him on a foreign mission field, for others in a church setting, and for many more it means confronting humanity in the public market places of the world.

In my conversation with a Native American and asking if he knows Jesus Christ as his personal Savior, his face lit up beaming with enthusiasm as he responded, "Oh! You know the Great Spirit as I do!"

God invites all men everywhere to discover Him as a personal friend through Jesus Christ and encourages all men to seek Him while He may be found. As the Great Spirit, the Almighty God, and the everlasting Father or as God told Moses, *"I Am, that I Am."*

"God is our refuge and strength, a very present help in time of trouble,"

(Psalm 45:1).

We will never discover our true identity and the person we are meant to become until we discover our life in Christ. Did you ever wonder why is it that millions of people die and the world will soon forget them, while others become immortalized and books are written about their accomplishments?

Following ones demise, the life of every person always stands as a record of who they were and what they did with their life, since life is as a vapor in time compared to eternity.

We are wise in seeking the Lord and to commit our life to live for Him and for His purpose and glory.

"Seek the Lord while He may be found, call upon Him while He is near. Let the wicked forsake his way, and the unrighteous man his thoughts; let him return to the Lord and He will have mercy on him; and to our God, for He will abundantly pardon. For my thoughts are not your thoughts, nor are your ways My ways, says the Lord. For as the heavens are higher than the earth, so are My ways higher than your ways, and My thoughts than your thoughts,"

(Isaiah 55:6-9).

Not knowing how to pray or what it meant to have a personal relationship with God was something that I greatly desired. From early childhood my desire to know God and His will for my life kept increasing more and more as I sensed an awareness of an inner voice speaking into my spirit; I had a desperate longing to know who God is.

However, I did not realize then that my search to know God would bring the forces of opposition against me from every direction attempting to deprive me of His will for who I believed I was meant to become. How could an uneducated simple Amish boy who spoke Pennsylvania Dutch be chosen to become an international radio voice to broadcast the gospel that would be heard by millions in many parts of the world?

It became obvious that God was indeed calling me into a relationship and I was soon made aware of the enemy's attempt to rob me of what would become the greatest blessing and adventure of my life, to walk with Jesus on assignment for world evangelism, taking me to some of the most remote areas of souls seeking a relationship with the true God of heaven. I was indeed called to proclaim the message of salvation, to invite individuals to come to the foot of His cross and accept Jesus Christ as Savior and Lord.

I had only discovered Jesus Christ at the age of twenty three after Anna Mary and I were married. A desire within me to experience the new birth intensified but I had no understanding of how to pursue such an experience nor did I realize the long road ahead in my search for spiritual fulfillment. Someone had given me a copy of the gospel of John and the story of Nicodemus remained a mystery to me, every chance I had I would slip away hiding somewhere to re-read the passage still not knowing what it meant to be born-again.

A Powerful Force Overwhelmed Me

One day while working in the cornfield I experienced a powerful presence coming upon me that was far greater than anything I had ever known. I had an urgent desire to pray, only twelve years old and having never been taught how to pray an audible prayer other than, *"Now I lay me down to sleep."* the words that were now coming from my lips seemed to flow from somewhere inside of me like a fountain overflowing, giving me a strange feeling of what was taking place. A spiritual force overtook me, and as I prayed thousands of black faces appeared before me, their countenance was very sad, they seemed to be reaching towards me with a desire for something I had to offer, even though I had no idea what that was. I remember a strange soft breeze blowing over my face and a voice inside of me telling me that I would someday be a missionary to many people. My first reaction was to tell my mother, her first response was, "do not talk to your father about this," so I kept my experience concealed all through my teenage years.

Thirty years later while on the island of Antigua in the West Indies I would again see those same faces in reality as I was preaching to a crusade crowd of five thousand black people who were now raising their hands in surrender to accept Jesus Christ as their personal Savior; that same gentle breeze was again blowing over my face with a strange presence and I knew without a doubt that I was in the presence and perfect will of God, the Holy Spirit had completely overtaken me to the extent that my black brothers had to help me stand on my feet trembling as I witnessed for the first time in my life hundreds of people coming to know Jesus Christ as their personal Savior.

I led them in the sinner's prayer, confessing Jesus Christ as their Savior and later followed up by sending many Bibles and gospel literature all over the West Indies islands and West Africa that my friends helped to sponsor. This would be the beginning of more crusades to the West Indies for the years ahead including Jamaica and Trinidad, and to also help sponsor and dedicate a church building for one of my pastor friends in Trinidad and years later help to sponsor a House of Prayer in the tribal regions of southeast India.

During my childhood years I was often kept out of school because of sickness. In spite of having no formal training and with no more than a simple elementary education the Lord would take me into remote areas of the world.

I had never been to Sunday school nor had I heard the salvation message. The Amish preach in High German, Pennsylvania Dutch is their common language. I understood very little of what was said even though I would cry as I tried to put together the stories the preachers would tell about Joseph, Daniel and David who became my favorite Bible characters. I understood absolutely nothing about the power or anointing of the Holy Spirit in a person's life.

More and more I would learn how this good man wanted to become not only my heavenly Father but also my very best friend, not only with the ability to overcome the bad man, but to call me into a world-wide ministry for His glory. To leave the Amish meant that I would not only violate my parent's wishes and their plans for my life, I would also bring disgrace and deep hurt upon them. I would be refusing to accept the farm they had worked so hard to purchase for me in the heart of Lancaster County, Pennsylvania only to become shunned with feelings of rejection.

I would learn the reality of the deception of the bad man the devil. Spiritual warfare would become a continual battle as I became aware how the enemy would use people to hinder and work against my desire to know the Lord's perfect will for my life.

Since my parents did not give me their permission to leave the Amish and since I did not want to dishonor them, this was one of the ten commands that I did not want to violate knowing that I would never be able to admonish other people to honor their parents if I failed to honor my Dad and Mother.

As a result of all this I began to rebel, I learned how to play the fiddle when I was sixteen and became involved with the wrong crowd. I even rebelled in trying to accomplish my farm chores; it was my responsibility to take care of Dads second farm which he had purchased for me. Plowing with horses took forever especially as I watched our more modern neighbors take their big tractors to the field and complete in several hours what took days for me to accomplish. If I could rent one of those tractors and plow by the light of the moon no one would know, especially not Dad, but I was wrong, it was Dad who was called before the church to make a confession for what I had done, you might imagine I never did that again! Someone who does not understand the rigid ruling and ways of the Amish might think, "What's the big deal about using a tractor to plow?" Tractors in that day were forbidden to be used for farming which was thought of as being worldly and to violate that ruling meant to be disciplined by the church fathers.

At the age of twenty one I had a farm accident which severed my left arm, now I was no longer able to play the fiddle. The doctor informed my Dad that he would be amputating my arm saying, "Your boy will have to go through life with a stub." Dad looked at the doctor and in his firm voice said, "Doctor you're going to put the boys arm back together," the doctor replied, "I can't" —- Dad said, "Doctor you haven't tried." This would become not only my first personal miracle, but my greatest heritage from Dad, since the Holy Spirit would use my hands to pray over the sick anointing them with oil and taking their hand and affirming them in their confession of faith.

Even though I could no longer play the fiddle because my arm grew crooked in the plaster cast that I carried for over a year, unknown to me then was that I would again experience another miracle years later as a result of a fall breaking both my wrists while building our house in Tennessee. During that operation my left arm was restored to where I could again play any instrument. For the theme song for my radio broadcast I would play my twelve stringed guitar and sing, "O how I love Jesus," that song would be aired wherever our broadcasts were heard.

As a result of my Dad interceding for me encouraging the doctor to spare my arm all added to my respect for Dad and his wishes for me to stay with the Amish. How the Holy Spirit intervened and spoke into Dad's spirit I will never know. In an unexpected moment three years after we were married and while working on the farm Dad had purchased for me I saw Mother coming across the fields, she was wiping her tears as she approached me and informed me saying, "Dad said you should leave the Amish and follow your call to ministry. You must talk to the Mennonite Bishop today!"

On several occasions following Dads passing, I would ask Mother what made Dad change his mind, her only response was a sweet smile without a word spoken. What helped me more than anything to surrender my life to the Lord was the peace I felt within my spirit to accept the following Scripture passage.

"If anyone comes to Me and does not hate his [own] father and mother [in the sense of indifference to or relative disregard for them in comparison with his attitude toward God] [likewise] wife and children, brothers and sisters-[yes] and even his own life also - he cannot be My disciple. And whoever does not bear his cross and come after Me cannot be My disciple,"

(Luke 14:26-27 AMP).

New Life Always Comes Forth out of Death

Anna Mary and I had endured our first year of farming with little success; our first major heartbreak came about when her father suddenly passed away. Three of our dabble gray horses died, five of our dairy cows died, a number of our chickens that were ready for market died but the most heart-breaking experience of that first year was when the doctor came to the house during a snow storm to deliver our first baby telling us that the baby had died in the womb several weeks before birth.

It was a cold winter morning as I carried our beautiful black haired little boy to the family cemetery in that small casket, the only people there were Anna Mary's mother, my parents, a few relatives and the Amish preacher. Every step walking up the long hill through the deep snow to the burial site was a step of condemnation for me, I felt so condemned and lost.

Throughout this book I will share my story, how that we sold everything we had and moved our family to the foothills of the Smoky Mountains in northeast Tennessee, and how I was ordained to the ministry, how God's call on my life unfolded through the years, only by a miracle of God's grace would I again not only play the violin, but also build many musical instruments including over sixty violins.

That day when I became a new creation in Christ at the age of twenty six, I realized for the first time in a very real way what Jesus Christ had provided not only for me but for all those who believe, everlasting life in Christ and freedom from condemnation including a great spiritual adventure.

God always has people in place to help us find our way into His will. To make the transition from driving a horse and buggy to that of a car introduced a new way of life to us. Sunday mornings became especially meaningful with the new form of worship, the beautiful hymns and the inspired missionary teaching all helped to shape our lives for the years ahead.

Radio evangelist C.M.Ward was a well known radio preacher from Springfield Missouri that we would listen to on our way to church, when giving the invitation he also made the comment, "Come down the saw-dust trail of repentance and come to Jesus." I had no idea what the saw-dust trail was until we attended our first tent revival, which in those days were very prominent. Saw dust was spread on the ground as a path leading to the altar and now I understood; the evangelist was simply making an appeal for people to get out of their seats and move to the front as an indication they wanted to surrender their lives to Christ. Little did I realize that one day our voice would also be heard by people we would never meet in this life, to also become inspired, to surrender their lives to Jesus Christ.

Since I experienced forgiveness with a wonderful deliverance, forgiveness would become the main thrust and theme for my message wherever our voice was heard.

For years I was confronted with rejection, but in time I realized that rejection will never do its harmful work in our lives if we don't receive it. Jesus was rejected so that we might be accepted; our condemnation along with everything else that we struggle with in life becomes our victory through Jesus Christ as joint heirs with Him.

The Holy Spirit would use our voice over the air waves informing our audience that sinful humanity can be made righteous before a Holy God washed in the blood of the Lamb, to be free indeed and to someday see Him and to know Him as He is and to be like Him.

What a thrill to see the greatest miracle of all miracles happening before my eyes as souls continued to surrender their lives to Jesus Christ. While on my first missionary crusade to the island of Antigua in the West Indies in 1967, I realized the people that stood before me were the same faces I saw in my father's cornfield so many years ago would become the driving force that kept me committed to my assignment for years to come. The joy coming from deep within their souls as they accepted Jesus Christ as their personal Savior, gave me the greatest soul-joy any Christian could hope for. Some of these people I would later commission to also preach the gospel of Jesus Christ.

As I witnessed the results of preaching the gospel, I realized how important the message of forgiveness was to God; since it is His forgiveness that sets us free from the bondage of sin and spiritual death. This would become the central theme for my message. Even though I didn't understand it then, but to tell this story is what was conceived within my spirit at an early age when my life was changed forever. I decided that whatever sacrifices I had to make to allow God to shape and prepare my life for the future is something I must do no matter what the cost, even if it meant leaving my Amish faith and their way of life to discover the call that God had placed upon me.

My prayer is that as we share our story, our readers will be encouraged to follow the Lord no matter what the cost involved and to follow the call God has placed upon your lives to become all you can be for Jesus Christ, for God's glory, and to never accept rejection, and no matter what you are facing now to realize that everything about God is supernatural, even though God is very busy with all He has to do. He has time to come into your situation and circumstances, providing you with a miracle of His grace, "just give God a chance!" Come to Him as you are so you can go forth as He is!"

Never Accept Rejection

One of my greatest struggles in leaving the Amish was to realize the consequences of knowing I would be expelled and excommunicated from the Amish church. That meant, I would become disowned and shunned by people I loved, which in time, resulted in feelings of worthlessness and rejection.

When a member violates a church ordinance or leaves the church they are excommunicated from the church body, the bishop will quote the passage from Paul's letter to the Corinthians,

> *"Deliver such a one to Satan for the destruction of the flesh, that his spirit may be saved in the day of the Lord Jesus,"*

(1 Corinthians 5:5).

This charge takes place before the entire congregation. The purpose is to encourage the one being excommunicated to repent and become reinstated rather than becoming lost to the world.

Feelings of condemnation and worthlessness followed me for a long time. The enemy would use this charge against me even though it was never meant to be a curse pronounced upon me, it had the same results. One night following a dream, I woke up terrified as I jumped out of my bed, I saw intense flames of fire, and thought I had gone to hell, with perspiration all over my body I knelt by my bed and prayed the best I knew how. This is not what I had experienced in the cornfield years earlier. I had felt so peaceful then and so close to God, now I felt so lost! Lord, "what does it mean to be born again?" I wrestled with that thought through the night, "God who are you, I want to know who you are?"

A teacher in our local town gave us Amish boys' weekly music lessons. One day he had a heart attack and was heard to say, "Oh No! I took care of everything but my soul!" and than he died. I did not want to die like that; but how can I know that I won't go to hell when I die?

Exhausted and still kneeling by my bed trying to pray, apparently the Lord heard my prayer and had mercy on me because I woke up later on from the most beautiful dream I ever had. I saw beautiful colored buildings so different from anything I had ever seen, it was like having taken a trip into heaven itself. I didn't see people, just beautiful buildings. As an artist I understand color but I have never painted with pigments or hues that were this beautiful, "but who could I tell since no one would understand." Not until years later as I listened to a friend share her story with me of what she saw as the result of her life after death experience my dream was confirmed.

My breakthrough moment came when my brother Mel invited me to attend a gospel crusade. I had never experienced anything like this before. The hymns touched my soul, the message convicted my heart, and the Holy Spirit moved my feet to the altar, and I was the first person to respond to the invitation to receive Jesus Christ as my personal Savior.

God Provides us with
Spiritual Significant Others

One of the highlights of my Christian life has been for the Lord to provide me with a spiritual life companion in the faith. Anna Mary has been a faithful wife and together we have become not only soul-mates but also intercessory prayer partners. On a missionary trip to the Dominica Republic while preparing to process through the ticket line at Dulles International Airport, we were asked what our purpose is in going to that part of the world. My response was that we were with a work and witness team from our church, but it was also our forty-seventh wedding anniversary. The lady at the ticket counter reacted by saying, "You're lying, no one is married that long today." When she realized that we were serious she called for an assistant who also asked me to confirm what I had just stated. She tore up our tickets. We had absolutely no idea of what they were doing until one of them said, "You're flying first class today, compliments of American airlines, and have a good flight!"

Together we sat in the first class section and were treated with honor and were asked to stand by the cockpit door as all the passengers deplaned including our team, wishing us a Happy Anniversary. In addition to that, we were asked to step into the cockpit for a photo with the flight crew.

While in flight to our destination and reflecting on the years we were together in ministry the Lord reminded me of how He had spared Anna Mary's life. It was our third year serving as a pastoral team in Tennessee when Anna Mary was diagnosed with a severe illness. The doctor told me I should prepare myself for the worst, he continued by saying,

"I will not be able to perform surgery since her body is too weak and it would be too dangerous."

Sitting on the side of her bed, Doctor Tate took her hand and began to pray, "Lord I cannot operate on this woman; if I take a knife to her body she might not recover, so I am asking You to heal this body in the name of Jesus."

Doctor Tate informed us to come back in three months for an evaluation when he would again examine Anna Mary. In the meantime, many of our friends and family, including our international radio audience joined with us in prayer and before the three months were up we noticed a big change in her condition. When we reported to the doctor following his examination, he informed us of the miracle that had taken place.

Meeting the Man who led me to Christ

It wasn't until twenty seven years later following our move from Tennessee to Virginia while attending seminary that I would meet the evangelist that led me to the Lord. I was preparing a term paper in the library of Eastern Mennonite University when I noticed a tall man that resembled the evangelist I had met years earlier. I introduced myself and asked, "Are you Myron Augsburger?" I shared in detail following my conversion, how the Lord led us as a family to pastor a congregation in northeast Tennessee and during that first year we were invited to broadcast the gospel on a local radio station which soon grew to an international ministry, broadcasting on Radio West Africa, The Gospel Voice of the Eastern Caribbean located on the island of St. Martin, Radio Paradise from the island of St. Kitts, World-Wide Christian Radio in Nashville, and stations State-side. Our God moment together that day wiping tears as we rejoiced became a memorial experience for both of us.

Our broadcasts were sponsored by various churches and individuals, therefore, we never asked for funds from our listening audience. Following twenty five years of broadcasting, we felt that door was closing as we spent more time in our counseling ministry. Ten years following our last broadcast, we were still receiving mail from overseas.

I graduated from seminary in 1987 with a Master of Arts degree in Church Ministries and Christian counseling. Counseling would open a new understanding of what it means to process forgiveness and to never accept rejection as we assisted struggling people find their way out of their crises situations to freedom in Christ.

An awesome awareness opened up to us with a new understanding of God's Word as we searched the scriptures. The more I pursued my relationship with the Lord, the more He revealed to me some of my weaknesses and inconsistencies. Placing our past behind us beccomes one of our greatest challenges, and unless we place our past completely under the blood of Jesus, we will be greatly hindered in our effective service for Christ. Through the maturing process, the Holy Spirit will refine us, making us aware of those inconsistencies so that we will confess them and place them under the blood of Jesus to receive complete forgiveness and deliverance. Failing to do so would result in our becoming paralyzed spitiually.

There are times when individuals fail the Lord and they seemingly cannot forget their past. It was in those moments that I heard the Lord saying, "If you can't receive and accept all that I did for you on My cross; all I provided for you by My death and resurrection from the dead, you are saying that was not sufficient for your need." This soon changed my attitude— —as I realized again in a new way, His grace was and always will be sufficient. I received what He did for me in a new way.

Do you realize that it takes more energy and effort to let go of our past failures in releasing those things that hinder us than it does to carry them with us through life as excess baggage. It is for this very reason that many people leave this world carrying heavy burdens with them to their graves rather than simply casting their burdens upon the Lord.

"Therefore humble yourselves under the mighty hand of God, that He may exalt you in due time, casting all your care upon Him, for He cares for you,"

(1 Peter 5:6-7).

How to Forget
What we don't want to Remember

We don't have to live where we were hurt or where our spirit was wounded. We don't have to replay the tapes and videos of our past memories to keep our mind informed of what took place. In our counseling ministry this is a problem source that will always surface, horrible childhood memories of abuse, or the abuse of a failed marriage or other hurtful relationships including not being able to forgive.

Only the Holy Spirit can enable us to delete and no longer dwell on those things we want to forget. Memory is a part of who we are; confession is the best antidote to forgetting and placing our past behind us that hinders our future. The apostle Paul had every reason for bad memories and has provided us with a Word to overcome whatever we wish to place behind us.

In his onslaught of killing innocent Christians, I'm sure he was reminded of those horrible moments now that he was a new creation in Christ. He gave us these powerful words to assist us in forgetting what we don't want to remember,

"...but one thing I do, forgetting those things which are behind and reaching forward to those things which are ahead, I press toward the goal for the prize of the upward call of God in Christ Jesus,"

(Philippians 3:13-14).

Chapter Three

Celebrating God's Presence

As we pioneered into new frontiers, the years that followed would be kind to us; our ministry would open doors of opportunity and understanding of how to come into God's presence by learning to wait until we heard His voice. By waiting on the Lord, we always learn the value of solitude and wisdom, but most of all listening to His voice. Our mind can find a place of rest from the frustrations of life by being alone with the Lord.

For most Christians, life has been an up and down cycle but we keep pressing on no matter what obstacles we face; the Lord will either make a way around, over the top, or right through since He promised to be our way-maker. We press towards our goal refusing to give up; hoping that tomorrow will be kinder than what we experienced yesterday.

For years I missed out on the blessing of simply listening; both to the Lord and to people. Growing older has its merit; our search to know the Lord better increases with time and we grow into a quality of life that is less hurried, we take more time to evaluate as we learn to observe while we listen. In my search to know the Lord in a more intimate way, as I found myself growing older, I decided to spend time in prayer until I received an answer. My prayer strategy was that I would fast and pray everyday, and all day, even into the night until I received an answer. Many days of fasting and praying all day, and three months into praying, I only discovered the art of listening. My breakthrough moment came while being totally exhausted by my many words to become completely still as I laid on the floor weeping, in my spirit I heard the words, "I turned My pain into a passion for My cross!" Where did those words come from? I didn't even have to write them down to remember them. I lay there on the floor in my tears having never experienced anything so profound before and still listening. "Now turn your pain into a passion, with compassion and you will discover your purpose!" For the next six months and everyday I wrote on the subject of intercessory prayer; a work that has since evolved into more than a thousand pages.

For two years I would be teaching in my Sunday school class what I learned during those listening days as I kept a journal of the voice that kept speaking into my spirit. The harvest that came out of that was my class becoming so involved in intercessory prayer that today there stands as a testimony of our passion together with compassion for lost people— — —a House of Prayer in southeast India.

My Thoughts are far Ahead of My Pen

The foothills of the Great Smoky Mountains are absolutely beautiful; especially in the fall of the year. From our mountain home in Tennessee, we had a thirty mile panoramic view of the North Carolina Mountain range with less than an hours drive to Grandfather Mountain and Linville Falls. These scenic locations provided me with an excellent environment to spend the day conversing with the Lord.

To observe an eagle soaring on the currents of the wind would always lift my spirit higher and I felt drawn closer to the Lord as a result of realizing once more His majestic power in creating such a beautiful world.

Many times my mind would go back to that day when God had revealed Himself to me as a small boy. So much of my life had changed. Back then, I hardly knew who God was; years of searching for Him changed all that. He was revealing so much of Himself to me so soon and so very real, the person soaring high above me on a hang-glider could not feel any freer than I did. I have been set free in my spirit to become more than I had ever hoped to be, and my childhood longings to know God were all coming into place more and more. I am now soaring in the realm of the Spirit touched by the hand of God. I know I'm in His will, my heart is in rhythm with His heart and pulsating with enthusiasm and we are the best of friends. The birds are singing their songs, there is a carefree atmosphere in the air, and the smell of the mountains is all around me with the beauty of the wildflowers. All this results in my thoughts being far ahead of my pen as I continue to journal my inspiration that I would be sharing with my listening audience. Just as I am being touched by the Holy Spirit my listening audience would feel that same anointing upon their lives setting us free to live for Him.

To be free from the ball and chain that had bound us; we are no longer victims of sin, and habits, to be made free indeed! And to only have thoughts of love and forgiveness. God, I feel like shouting. There is so much of my life behind me and so much living before me and to think of all that is prepared in eternity for those who will follow Jesus in obedience is beyond our human comprehension.

Following my trips to the mountains, spending time with the Lord better prepared me for the responsibility and challenge in ministry that was still to come. I would have to speak encouraging words into hearts that were troubled, even to individuals that had little time to live; some of these people were not prepared to die.

I would witness individuals accepting Jesus as their Savior before taking their last breath; I also witnessed others leaving this world unprepared to die, fighting the flames of hell as they died. If you are not prepared to meet the Lord, now would be a good time to turn to the prayer at the end of this book praying the sinner's prayer and asking Jesus to come into your heart. It takes less than thirty seconds of our time to confess Jesus Christ as our personal Savior. As Christians, we all know it involves our entire life to live out our confession of faith, but our life with Christ only begins as we repent from our sins and ask Jesus to come into our heart and save our soul. Jesus is always waiting for that moment when an individual decides to surrender to His love, mercy and grace, and He will abundantly pardon from any and all transgression to give us eternal life.

Discovering Our Ultimate Potential

God always asks for our best, to work at the discovery of our ultimate potential, this may include forsaking everything that has become important to us only to discover things we had never known or understood before. For many people it involves leaving friends and family, moving to a whole new environment and culture, to discover other people and becoming the best of friends. By giving up something that we cherish dearly always results in gaining those things we never knew existed. Whatever it is that we must leave behind, to lose our life for Christ is to not only gain His favor and blessing, but we are taken into a world of activity we had never before experienced.

Our Faith in God and hope for what seems impossible will enable us to strive toward our intended goals, hope alone cannot thrive by itself; this is why our faith in God, our fellowman, including ourselves becomes important to accomplish our seemingly impossible goals.

One good analogy concerning faith and hope as becoming one would be that of a violin. Since I have crafted numerous violins and discovered that the violin in and by itself cannot produce music, just as faith without hope cannot touch the depth and the passions of our heart to produce a spiritual quality of life. Only as the bow makes contact with the strings can a violin produce music from within, as hope makes contact with our faith, our spirit and soul become overwhelmed with the passions of our heart and faith calls forth from out of the depth of our heart to achieve its desired goals, unless rosin is applied to the bow there is no music, rosin is an oil substance symbolic of the Holy Spirit in our lives.

The Holy Spirit makes our hope in everything that God is alive. Hope is not wishful thinking, but rather hope expresses the intent, our desire and the deep longings of our soul which consists of mind, will, and emotion. The sound post within the violin located beneath the bridge which carries the sound through the sound post and vibrates from the back of the instrument and through the F-holes on the top is referred to as the soul or the emotion of the violin.

A master violinist can produce sound that holds the attention of an audience for hours on end. On the other hand, the violin in the hands of the amateur can empty a building in a matter of minutes since there are no pleasing sounds, just a disturbing noise. The same applies to our soul; unless it becomes transformed by the Holy Spirit it remains corrupt, incomplete and disturbing to many people. Hope serves as a sound-post to our persistent refusing to let go faith, the kind of faith that will not only move mountains, but a faith that has an attractive appeal to its audience.

Cross-culture experiences add to our faith, both in God and in the people we hope to reach for Christ, such experiences are always challenging in refining our faith which helps us to refine our personality with a new awareness of the world around us, providing us with even greater Kingdom activities we never knew existed.

For me this meant winning my first convert to the Lord. I will always remember the joy within my spirit, to see the radiance coming forth not knowing what battles were overcome by a new found relationship with Jesus Christ. These experiences only cause us to become more involved, we become so caught-up in the soul-winners joy that we are willing to sacrifice anything even our own life to help another individual find peace with God in friendship evangelism activities.

As an extension of my ministry, I decided to open a school of art in our town, individuals would come into my studio to look around and admire my paintings commenting, "I wish I could do that!" My response always was, "you can become anything you desire to be on two conditions, if you are willing, and if you follow instructions." It wasn't long until I had more than thirty students enrolled for weekly two hour sessions with classes every day of the week. In time, I realized I was leading more people to the Lord in my art studio than I was at the church where I served as pastor and I wondered what made the difference, then I discovered that not until we win the trust of another person are we able to win their confidence and when we do that they want to share even the deep secrets of their struggles to find freedom in forgiveness through a right relationship with Christ.

My art studio was located right next to the funeral home; it was not unusual for the funeral director to call me on a moments notice to conduct the service for the family that obviously had no pastor. For this reason, I kept a black suit and a Bible handy, this also placed me in touch with many new people that I would other wise never have met to also challenge their spirituality. During a graveside service, even though the crowd was quite large I suggested that we sing, "What a Friend We Have in Jesus." I found myself to be the only one singing. On another occasion when I entered the funeral parlor the large family was seated in a large circle. I had learned to wait until the director gave me the nod to begin the usually short service. The man opposite me got my attention with his stern look especially when he stood up and stepped in front of me asking, "are you the preacher?' I informed him that I was, in an authoritative voice he informed me, "Now we don't want a long sermon, do you understand that!" I assured him that I did. Apparently he wasn't confident, for the third time he stood in front of me informing me of his wishes. For a mediation I would usually use the twenty-third Psalm, I got carried away with my inspiration and thirty minutes went by before I realized I had taken so long. Later that day one of the family came by our house to thank me for the meditation telling me it was just what the gentleman needed.

My large store-front windows along main-street displayed my paintings; it was not unusual for out-of- state people who were traveling through the Smoky Mountain's to stop by and enjoy my art. I had just returned from an educational trip to Europe and after visiting the many cathedrals I was inspired to paint my version of the three crosses. The man that rushed into my studio early one morning informed me that he was a part of a large church in Lynchburg, Virginia, and the large painting on display was meant just for him. Without hesitation he informed his wife, "Pay the man!" On another occasion, just for the fun of it I painted a pair of mules I remembered from the farm, they had now been hanging on my studio wall for more than a year without capturing anyone's interest. One day I had an idea and decided to title the painting. On a readable plate from the outside sidewalk I engraved the title, "The Town Jack-butts." It was late Saturday night when I received the call from a man who said, "I'm an evangelist in town holding revival meetings and my pastor friend and I went out for a stroll and looked in your studio windows

— please don't sell that painting, I will be in you shop early Monday morning to pick it up, I know those boys!"

My counseling ministry would eventually lead me to a seminary in Virginia to work toward a degree in Christian counseling. This move would in turn open even more doors of opportunity to serve the Lord, but mostly in the public market place where both Anna Mary and I felt called to become encouragers and friends to those who either misunderstood the established church, or who became wounded by the professing church, having fallen through the cracks left bleeding and dying.

Jesus came for sinners and to invite them to repentance. He came for those who were lonely, depressed and without hope. The hell's angel type of man who parked his big motorcycle caught my attention. He is now sitting down at the restaurant table having apparently lost his macho image. I thought these guys were hardhearted and tough. Joining him with a cup of coffee I said, "I see a lot of hurt in your eyes, would you like to talk about it?" His fist hit the table getting the attention of all those who were present. He told me of his depression, just wanting to die, even hoping to have a fatal wreck on his ride that day. "I've never been to this place in my life, I just felt led to stop in for a cup of coffee and you sit down and ask me, do you want to talk about it. Yes! I want to talk about it." Less than an hour later that same man was a brand new man and all he needed was for someone to listen and give him simple instruction and direction to bring meaning and purpose into his life.

Earlier experiences with people had taught me valuable lessons that could be applied for life, which was to accept individuals for who they were as they were, including the spiritual condition they might find themselves. Jesus always accepted people at face value no matter what condition they were in to move them beyond that situation into hope and freedom with love and forgiveness providing them with self esteem and purpose.

The middle aged couple we met in the market place both seemed distraught. The lady looked sad, yet she had a beautiful smile in spite of her one eye being at least one inch above the other; the gentleman was obviously bitter. When I asked him what he did for a living he responded by saying in a loud voice, "I'm a preacher, and I'm mad at God!"

"I asked him, why are you mad at God?" he then went on to explain the health problems his wife had encountered, a tumor was pushing her eye out of place. "Why would God kill my wife after serving Him faithfully all these years, and why would God take our children's mother away from them when they need her the most?"

What a challenge to minister into an emotional hurt and to become involved with complete strangers. "You're not mad at God," I said, your hurt is so deep you don't know how to express yourself." I went on to ask him the question, "how many times have you told other people to cast all their cares upon Jesus and now that it's your turn you don't know how to do that." He agreed I was right.

I challenged both husband and wife to make a covenant agreement, calling everyone that we both knew to pray that God's will be done, they agreed. Since I had an international audience for prayer partners and many local friends, along with all the people they would contact we committed ourselves to prayer.

I thought we would see them in several weeks, but several months went by before we saw them again, as they entered the market place I noticed the lady's eyes were straight and she had a big smile, her husband also looked completely different. "What happened?" I asked, they explained that in their desperation they had traveled to Europe and Mexico seeking medical help and one morning as she looked into the mirror she noticed her eye was normal. After consulting their doctor, they were informed that the Lord had indeed performed a miracle. In the meantime, they had resigned their pastorate position.

Not until two years later did we see them again, by now they had moved to another State and were both involved in new ministries. The lady was in demand to speak at Aglow meetings and her husband found a new form of ministry as well. There was no more bitterness and coldness toward God.

Had the Holy Spirit not prepared me for this moment in time, if I had harbored bitterness myself, or an unforgiving spirit in my heart I would have missed these confrontations with people, failing to seize the moment and these people may never have found their way because someone was not there for them. God has each and every person planted at specific geographical locations to be a witness for Him and some of these places may be the most undesirable places and situations that we would never choose ourselves.

My first involvement in church ministries would not be confronting hell's angel's type guys. To see the hurt in the eyes of people, I would learn my elementary lessons in working with people by teaching a class of fourteen year old boys. One of those boys was rowdy, even cruel at times poking his lead pencil into the leg of the person sitting beside him, and if they cried he was delighted. Following such an incident, I took Lee outside into the stair well of the church. In my spirit, I wanted to punish him; but in my heart, I felt the need to love him by saying, "Lee you are a great guy and the Lord has great plans for you in the future." I had no idea then how those words would become real later in life and how I would reap a harvest in my time of need. Years went by and I no longer thought of Lee until he called me saying— —I heard you fell and broke both of your wrists, I want to come and help you anyway that I can.

By now I was producing radio broadcasts that reached many remote areas of the world, our house was under construction and there was so much work to be done and I am now completely incapacitated. I could do absolutely nothing. Lee became my hands to push the controls on the consol from where we produced our radio programs, he became my hands for everything I needed to do including driving me where I needed to go, turning the pages of my Bible, signing my name. Lee stayed with us until I was able to drive again and use my hands to produce my broadcasts and without any reimbursement. In time Lee got married and together he and his wife were sent to the mission field and I was thankful that I had not wounded his spirit with unkind words. That class of boys taught me invaluable lessons in working with other people after I became a pastor.

Our brokenness, brings forth His Redemption

While in the hospital recuperating from my shattered wrists and in great pain in spite of all the morphine, a nurse came into my room and said, "We need you down the hallway, please come right away!" An old man was at the point of death. His wife had heard that someone with both arms in cast had been going around the hospital rooms praying for people. The lady informed me that her husband was ninety years old and not a Christian. In a trembling voice she asked, "Would you please talk with my husband, he never lived one day for the Lord. I can't bear to see him die in this condition, he can hear you alright but he cannot make any sounds." I spoke to the man as if he were a child, telling him how much Jesus loves him and if he wanted to become a Christian before he goes into eternity, that I would pray the sinner's prayer, then I said, "No matter what you have done or didn't do, Jesus wants to save your soul and what matters now is not what you did, but that you surrender your heart asking

Jesus to forgive you and save your soul and that he should indicate to me his decision by squeezing my finger.

With both arms in cast and only one finger that I could move, I placed it into the old man's hand, his wife and the nurses who were standing behind me began to praise the Lord. I looked around and asked, "How did you know?" Her response was, "It was the look that came over his face, I have never seen him look so peaceful in all my life," the old man soon passed away.

By this experience, I was certain why the Lord allowed all this to take place at this time in my life. Had I not been there on location the old man might have gone into eternity without knowing the Lord. I was also made aware again of how Jesus suffered for us so that we might be made free from sin and have eternal life and how He wants us to become an extension of who He is in the world today even if that means going through severe bodily or soul pain. Our brokenness many times conditions us for the task He desires us to perform for Him. In our quest to discover who God is, we learn to know Him in a more intimate way through the experiences that life offers to us and we learn to become an extension of who He desires to be in us, in the world today.

God wants to be known. He desires for every individual to discover Him in a personal relationship through Jesus Christ. He wants us to experience His power through the Holy Spirit and this is why He presents us with diversified opportunities of discovery. He desires to become intimate with us, not a distant remote God, but close and personal, as real as the air we breathe.

God wants us to experience His holiness, His purity, to know His Word which He always puts above His name with a sure promise of blessing for our obedience. His Word is a revelation of everything God is, His arms are always open to receive us just as we are.

Even though our confession is important, He is even more interested in loving us back to Himself. What He can do for us means more to Him than what we did or do against Him. He is not willing that anyone perish without knowing him, but that all men would repent from their sins, to come as we are, so He can send us forth as He is for His purpose and glory.

The Gospel is the Power of God unto Salvation

Preaching the gospel provided me with many soul-winning opportunities; I had absolutely no understanding of the dynamics involved in radio broadcasting. I would in time, however, realize the far reaching effects it would have by impacting listeners in many parts of the world.

During our first year in Tennessee, one of my friends from my former Sunday school class encouraged me to broadcast on our local radio station saying he would sponsor the cost involved. In time, that resulted in other Sunday school classes from other churches helping with the costs. This is why I never had to make an appeal for funds from my listening audience for the twenty five years we were on the air without listener support which made our broadcasts very unique.

"Where are the black faces I wondered?" My experience in the corn field was very real and there were hardly any African Americans living in our area. But I was soon to discover what the Lord had in mind with that vision. As I turned the pages of a Christian Magazine my eyes fell on the advertisement, "Old fashioned Gospel Broadcasters wanted on Missionary Station in the West Indies, send tape for audition." Immediately I knew God wanted us on that station. Our audition tapes were accepted with the manager saying, "Send us your tapes right away; we have reserved a nightly spot for you on our program log."

Making live broadcasts was one thing, but to learn how to properly tape a program on a recorder was altogether different for me. I built my own console with the help of a Christian friend who was experienced in radio broadcasting; we produced our programs in the back of the chapel where I served as pastor and in time constructed a building for radio production.

My script was in front of me and I had played two opening songs and was well into my message when someone knocked on the back door. This meant I had to stop and answer the knock at the door. A neighbor wanted to borrow a shovel. I accommodated the request and again started from the beginning only to be interrupted again having encountered a coughing spell. My third interruption resulted when the top reel fell off the console and unto the floor rolling down the isle of the church.

Now, I was not only disgusted, I had lost all my inspiration. So I did what I always did before, I shared my problems with Anna Mary, "I quit!" I said as I walked in the door, "What's wrong now," she asked. I told her of my frustration telling her I would wait until tomorrow, "but your tapes have to be in the mail today to arrive at the station on time." She was right; it took three weeks for a tape to arrive on the island of St. Maartin, in the West Indies from where the programs were aired.

"Let me pray for you," she said. That, in time, became my lifeline and together we would learn the value of spending time together asking the Lord to make a way for what seemed like impossible situations.

Since I had lost all inspiration, I sat there before the consol and out of habit reached for my guitar. As I strummed over the strings a tune came to mind that the young people were singing at that time. I decided to use the message of the song for my broadcast, so I began to sing.

The lyrics told of Jesus walking upon the scene when the woman taken in adultery was about to be stoned and how He accepted her for who she was, as she was, challenging the religious leaders concerning their own life by saying, *"He that is without sin among you let him throw the first stone,"* and then to tell the woman that in Him there is no condemnation, and when Jesus asked the woman where her accusers were, and if no one had condemned her, she responded by saying, *"No one Lord."* Jesus then said, *"Neither do I."* When the woman acknowledged Jesus as Lord, the Holy Spirit transformed her heart.

For the next several programs I spoke from this text and only the Holy Spirit would know what prompted me to pick up my guitar and sing that song that day. Three weeks later, and thousands of miles away on a tropical island in the West Indies, five young girls were traveling on their way to a night club where they worked as prostitutes. Their car broke down and while four of the girls went looking for help Ellen stayed with the car to protect their belongings. Not knowing what time it was, Ellen turned on the car radio, just at the very moment my broadcast was being aired from another island hundreds of miles away. "Neither do I condemn thee." was coming over the airwaves loud and clear, and anointed by the Holy Spirit which lodged the message deep within Ellen's heart and soul with conviction.

Our very first air mail letter from the West Indies arrived six weeks following that initial broadcast from someone by the name of Ellen Pamperton, the following excerpts are from that letter.

Dear Brother David,

I was traveling with four of my friends. We were on our way to a hotel where we worked to do what us girls did, the car broke down and while my friends were looking for help I stayed with the car to protect our belongings, knowing we would be late for our appointment. I turned on the car radio to check the time, your program had just come on and you were singing the song, "Neither do I condemn thee go and sin no more," and then you continued for the next twenty minutes talking about that subject. You said that no matter how deep in sin a person may go, Jesus will always forgive and transform our lives into a new creation. I was so convicted of my sins that when we arrived at the hotel I asked my manager if I could stay in my room that I wasn't feeling well. He allowed me to do that and throughout the night I thought about what you had said. The next evening, I again requested to stay in my room and when your program came on the radio I again listened to you as you continued speaking on this same subject and when you gave the invitation I asked Jesus to come into my heart.

Ellen

Ellen continued to write to us every week for the next year. She would share about the Sunday school class she was now teaching. Every letter she sent, we realized how much she was growing in her relationship with the Lord. The following year, I received an invitation to come to the island of St. Kitts and Nevis for a crusade.

I had never flown on an airplane before. For the first twenty six years of my life, I had traveled by horse and buggy driving around Amish country. It was twelve miles to Anna Mary's house and I drove there every weekend, summer, and winter no matter how deep the snow. I would always find my way to her house; sometimes I went in a one-horse open sleigh with bells ringing.

I had never conducted a crusade in my life, and Tennessee was the farthest I had ever traveled. Boarding the big jet plane at Knoxville all alone was quite an experience, "Why are airports so big, and what is meant by the Gates I wondered?" I asked a lot of questions on my flight to Miami and on to my final destination.

Following a rough landing with my Bible and guitar in hand, I was met by a group of black pastors who welcomed me as if I was coming home. How do all these people know my name I wondered! I was still trembling as a result of that small plane landing on the edge of the beach beside the palm trees.

As my new found friends escorted me to the ball park where the crusade was being held one of the men said, "Brother David, there are some folks here that are anxious to meet you, they are waiting for you at the top of the steps leading to the platform from where you will be preaching.

Standing at the top of the stairs were five young women with great big smiles. Their hands extended in welcome, the first one to speak said, "Brother David, I'm Ellen and these are my four friends. Ellen had won her four prostitute friends to Jesus and now they were sitting with the pastors' wives on the crusade platform; what a moment in time for this former Amish boy who had never been exposed to such beautiful black people. It seemed as if they smiled with their entire body.

As I was preaching to an estimated crusade crowd of around five thousand people, I suddenly became aware that the people I'm looking at are the same people that I saw in my father s corn field so many years ago. Now I understood why I saw those faces as if they were reaching towards me for something I had, and I didn't understand that, since all I saw were faces. Now I see their hands raised toward heaven in worship. I saw tears streaming down their faces as they responded to the invitation. They came forward by the hundreds; this would be my first experience in winning so many people to the Lord, Wow! What a moment!

I left those islands with an awesome sense and awareness of the power of the gospel, having worked through one of the most difficult times of my life, to leave my parents knowing I had broken their hearts.

I left the island of Nevis and flew via Haiti and on to Miami. The newspaper at the airport caught my attention as I read the bold headlines— — —Ferry capsizes between St. Kitts and Nevis, three hundred people perish in shark infested waters.

By the time I arrived home, I soon learned by the amount of mail we were receiving that many young people who had attended the crusade and had accepted the Lord were on that fatal Ferry and had perished. Then we received the shocking letter from someone who had known Ellen, who wrote to tell us that she too had perished on that Ferry. Even though the remains of their bodies are on the bottom of those Caribbean waters, their souls are rejoicing in the presence of the Lord. Jesus did not condemn those girls in spite of the lives they had lived, they heard a simple gospel message anointed by the Holy Spirit, and they responded to a simple invitation and found eternal Life in Jesus Christ.

This is the power of the gospel unto salvation for everyone who believes; Jesus is still sinner friendly; He always was and always will be. His story continues through time, transforming the hearts of sinners into children of His Kingdom. This is why Jesus came to earth to save sinners; it is what He does best. The story continues as long as its being told and countless lives are being changed from sinners to saints. Every time sinners respond to the invitation to surrender their lives to Jesus Christ, His grace is always sufficient to save them no matter how deep their sin.

Death for these girls and the way they died was not their enemy, it became their gateway into eternal glory, their short lives living as Christians redeemed from a life of sin stands as a record of God's redeeming grace. With the awesome reality that any one individual, no matter how deep in sin they may go, can receive Jesus Christ by faith through a simple message of the gospel and can be transformed and forgiven in a moment of time as new creations of God's grace.

Why is it that in the most unexpected moments the Holy Spirit prompts us to do what we had never thought of before? Could it be that He desires to confirm all that has transpired in a new way and to also reveal to us additional instructions for our continued ministry?

The Holy Spirit as our counselor, always has His way of bringing encouragement into our lives, providing us with a renewed determination to follow Him at all cost, to pursue uncharted and unconquered territory.

More then six decades had come and gone since that day when the Holy Spirit revealed my future, we were sitting around Mothers table celebrating her ninety eighth birthday and reminiscing about all the major events of our lives. "Do you remember the day when I shared my experience with you, and what happened for you and Dad to release me to follow my call to ministry?" I asked Mother. "And what prompted Dad to change his mind?" All these questions led us to reflect upon the many places we had traveled and the people we had met that had changed our lives and their lives forever.

For the first time in my life after all those years I had a desire to stand again on the very spot where the Lord had given me a vision of preaching to those thousands of black people.

Together Anna Mary and I along with brother Mel stood there under a beautiful blue sky similar to that of the very day I received my call to ministry, the clouds were again billowy white and we felt the presence of the Lord with us as we thanked Him for all that had taken place since that day including the harvest of souls that were born into the Kingdom of Christ.

It was a beautiful spring day; the Amish farmers were plowing new–ground, planting there crops to anticipate a bountiful harvest, across the fields we could see the family cemetery where we had buried our first child and where twenty years ago we had laid Dad to rest, it would be here that our bodies would also rest waiting the resurrection morning.

As we prayed together with hands raised toward heaven so much of our life unfolded before us like a movie screen, bringing back memories of the milestones of God's mercy, for this reason we wanted to establish a memorial there of how the Holy Spirit had touched our lives and led us to some of the remote areas of the world to preach the gospel.

Now we are challenged to commit our lives to the Lord in a renew way, to discover the plans He still has for us to accomplish, and to also plow new ground and plant the seeds of the gospel into the lives we would yet meet to anticipate a harvest for the Lord, with our ministry now being in the classroom, the prayer room, and the market-place. Hopefully as our story is shared from the printed page the Holy Spirit will yet produce the greatest harvest of all for the glory of Christ and His Kingdom.

Chapter Four

Jesus Identifies with our Tears

God created us as individuals to be on special assignment for Him; no other person can live our life, do our work or make our decisions. The early disciples were individually unique with individual giftedness with assignments and so are we. The Holy Spirit will bring certain people into our lives that we are meant to challenge, our mission is just that; not to condemn anyone for who they are or what they have done, but to challenge individuals with a gospel of love and invite them to Christ.

To discover our identity and assignment, the Lord always has other individuals in place to direct our path to discover ourselves in Him. It becomes important that we consult spiritual discerning individuals that will walk with us on our path of discovery as mentors. It becomes our responsibility to seek out those individuals that the Lord always provides, no matter where in the world we go, there is someone already there in place by God's divine providence that will help us to become what we were meant to be in Christ.

One of my great blessings in life has been the Lord providing me with mentors to help me develop my spirituality, my character, and personhood. Likewise He brought secular mentors into my life that helped me to develop my giftedness in art and music.

Everything we desire to become already lies within us, our obedience to Christ unlocks the door to everything God has planned for us to become. Before I became a Christian the Lord had spiritual significant others in place, this included Sunday school teachers, preachers and evangelists and a host of other individuals who always have a part in who we become as God's servants. We never mimic them, we develop into our own person, for God's glory, but the influence of these people became a part of who we become since we are always developing into more of who we are meant to be, but we don't have to follow someone else's formula in our style of worship, our prayer life or service.

Our future is more important than our past even though our past has allowed us to mature and develop into the person we are today. It was because of these persons that I became involved in the areas that now mean so much to me and has shaped my life forever.

The famed artist Rembrandt challenged his students to copy him knowing full well they would never equal him, Paul said, *"I follow after Christ,"* but Paul could never be Jesus, however, the life of Jesus and the power of Jesus would come forth by the Holy Spirit in him as Paul ministered in Jesus' name. Jesus Christ modeled His life according to His Father in heaven; He could do that because He was God in the flesh. The only way for us to succeed in life and in ministry is to model our lives according to Christ, not our heroes of faith even though they challenge us as mentors of our faith; this is why Paul said, *"Christ in you, the hope of glory."*

There is Power in the name of Jesus

I became involved in church activity in the day when the name of Jesus was still the main subject of every sermon with the emphasis on the power of His name including the power of the blood. Today that emphasis has changed in some churches. The name of Jesus is seldom mentioned and when that occurs there is no spiritual power. When that happens all that is left is a social gathering with no miracles taking place and few souls are coming into the Kingdom. God is honored only through the name of His Son.

I had compassionate mentors; therefore, I became a compassionate person in ministry. I had pastors and teachers that had a burden for lost people; this has become my passion in ministry. Our compassion for a hurting world will always speak for itself by our actions which will always draw individuals to us especially when they need direction, counsel or prayer.

We will never have a burden for lost people until we shed tears in their behalf, when we are broken in our spirit with compassion for those that are lost. The Lord will provide us with an audience. Jesus spent much time in prayer with His Heavenly Father; early in the morning He went away to a solitary place and when the disciples wondered why they could not perform miracles as he did, He challenged them to fast and pray.

Tears Wash Our Soul

Our greatest breakthrough always comes by our brokenness; Godly sorrow for our sin, including true repentance, sincere devotion and loyal service to the Lord. Our tears of repentance wash our soul, as we accept and receive forgiveness. Our tears keep us close to the cross, tears are a language all by themselves, the circumstances of life produce them and by them we express the emotions of our heart and soul, including our pain and disappointments. Tears also become an antidote for our pride.

A young pastor with his first assignment stepped up to the pulpit in all his pride and when words failed him as he stood before a congregation of people who were now staring at him, he finally broke down in tears, embarrassed having said absolutely nothing, he stepped off the platform and sat down by the old pastor who had recently resigned, the old pastor in his kind gentle way placed his hand on the man and said, "Young man, if you would have walked into the pulpit as you walked away from the pulpit, you would have had a message for the congregation."

Ministry is always birthed out of tears; tears flowing from out of our spirit will always touch the spirit of the one we are praying for even though we may be miles apart. Complacency and arrogance will never win people to Christ, but when we fast and pray, heaven opens up to us. Someone once said, "If we want our prayers answered the best thing we can do to bring about results is to answer someone else's prayer, we have tried this and it works.

Ministry caused me to become so involved that I had nearly forgotten Edith who came to me every Sunday while I was serving as Sunday school superintendent at our home church, and always with a face full of tears flowing out of her heart deeply burdened for the lost soul of her only son.

Years went by and one day we were informed that Edith had passed away; the doctor said she died from a heart attack, but I knew that she had died from a broken heart. One day her husband came home from work and found her by the bedside where she always knelt in prayer interceding for her lost son.

I had never met her son and was no longer praying for him since so many other things now occupied my mind. We were in need for summer Bible school teachers and made a request for a young couple to teach the youth group. When we arrived at the church there were only two young girls that attended, the other adults were older people. We decided to ask these girls to invite their school friends to meet us at the local school on Tuesday evenings for a ball game and then to have a Bible study at the Chapel including refreshments in our home. The first night to our surprise, there were more than forty young people who turned out for the game and they all came to the church for the Bible study. Many of these young people had not been involved in any church activity, but this in time would make up the congregation that is still being blessed today and growing after more than forty years through the effort of faithful followers of Jesus Christ. One of the former girls that helped us to start that youth ministry is the pastor's wife where they are faithfully serving the Lord and where she has now attended for more than forty years.

I didn't recognize the young couple that pulled into the church parking area of the Rainbow Chapel, the young man introduced his wife and then said, "I'm Ray, you might remember my mother Edith."

Ray and his wife were the most on-fire young couple that I had ever met, they served the Bible school with great dedication and witnessed throughout the community, and I knew that the prayers of a mother's heart that had been crushed with compassion for her lost son were answered. In time Ray and his wife were called to pastor a congregation and continued to be on fire for Jesus.

You might be able to identify with the burden Edith had for her lost child, if so, be persistent in prayer, never give up, intercessory prayer will reach the heart of God and He always has His right time moments to perform His work of redemption. Never give up and hold on to your faith and just keep on loving your loved ones, your tears will not be in vain!

Never underestimate your prayer power or your tears before God pleading for lost loved ones. The Holy Spirit will set them ablaze, and we never know what will come out of the travail of the soul, as we intercede for those who went astray.

When we speak prayer words into the atmosphere and they ascend as incense before God's throne, we will be amazed at the results of His favor and blessing, God preserves our tears in a bottle in heaven as a testimony of our compassion.

The ministry of Jesus today is interceding at the right hand of God, the old rugged cross is empty and so is His grave that could not hold Him. The price He paid for the redemption of a lost soul was too great to not continue as His greatest mission ever accomplished. What really happens when a mother or father go to be with Jesus? Could it be that they will join in the ministry of intercession for loved ones on the earth? Could it be that when Edith went to heaven she made an appeal to Jesus as intercessor to send the Holy Spirit into the life of her lost son joining the great cloud of witnesses? We can only imagine!

May Your Kingdom Come

People have strange ideas about what heaven will be like, just as with the gospel. Many people try to make heaven what it is not, to not receive it for what it is meant to be. We can only imagine, but there is nothing wrong with that, neither is there any harm in reading the revelation already provided as to what heaven will be like.

In sharing the beauty of heaven according to scripture with an individual who claimed to be a Christian, the individual remarked, "I don't really know that I look forward to sitting on a cloud playing a harp forever." People need to read the Bible; which provides descriptive details of what heaven will be like, including the activity of heaven, our activity with the King of Kings and Lord of Lords during the millennial reign. John provides in detail the size of the

New Jerusalem and the detailed beauty of the City of God including the New Earth.

One day Jesus will ride out of eternity on a white horse and the saints will follow Him also riding white horses; did you ever wonder what will become of all those white horses, will they disappear or will they also become a part of the landscape during the thousand year reign? In sharing that with someone, I was asked, "How do you know that?" My response was, "I read it in the Bible!"

"The wolf also shall dwell with the lamb, the leopard shall lie down with the young goat, the calf and the young lion and the fatling together; and a child shall lead them. The cow and the bear shall graze; their young ones shall lie down together; and the lion shall eat straw like the ox. The nursing child play by the cobra's hole, and the weaned child shall put his hand in the vipers den. They shall not hurt nor destroy in all My holy mountain, for the earth shall be full of the knowledge of the Lord as the waters cover the sea.

(Isaiah 11:6-9).

In light of all that Jesus is preparing for those who love Him, why should anyone decide to forfeit their salvation to live a life of sin and to never discover what Jesus has prepared for them, for all eternity saying,

"Eye has not seen, nor ear heard, nor have entered into the heart of man the things which God has prepared for those who love Him,"

(1 Corinthians 2:9).

A certain lady who had a life after death experience told of the sounds she heard as the angel gave her a tour of the Holy City of God, "what are the echoing sounds I hear?" she asked. The angel responded by informing the lady that the sounds she was hearing were the prayers of the saints that continue to live on to perform their work of redemption on the earth until the work is accomplished.

According to scripture there is a great cloud of witnesses in heaven that surrounds us, and we are instructed to be conscious of that. This heavenly host includes the Old Testament saints recorded in Hebrews (12:1). Why then would this cloud of witnesses not include our loved ones who have gone on to be with Jesus; the author and finisher of our faith, to accomplish His work of redemption on the earth, as He intercedes, with all of heaven's focus on His intercession, to witness the salvation process, as lost souls are redeemed by the power of His blood and of His cross.

This is where intercessory ministry is happening right now, at the right hand of the Father as Jesus prays for the lost souls on the earth. If we are going to be present with Him in heaven, why then, would we not also witness His mighty intercessory prayer power, and to also join in with our praise; especially when a lost person is redeemed by His blood, and by the convicting power of the Holy Spirit. God will be God and we cannot limit Him as to how He operates.

I can see a mother or father who has entered heaven's portals observing the intercessory ministry of Jesus. The great shouts of jubilation that echo throughout heaven when a sinner becomes redeemed on the earth.

I can only imagine Edith joining Jesus in interceding for her lost son, as she looks unto Jesus who promised that He would be, *"the author and finisher of her faith,"* according to Hebrews (12:2). Why should the death of our body cancel the spirit of our faith? Since Jesus Christ is the object and embodiment of our faith, including the perfection of our faith, and since He is the same yesterday, today and forever; why should our prayers on earth be cancelled the moment we enter heaven?

I believe that our prayers will continue to perform their work until the work is accomplished. Our prayers prayed in faith in the name of Jesus will pursue their objects into the unknown future until they accomplish their purpose. family circle's will be complete in heaven, and not one of our loved ones will be excluded, at least, we know they too are invited, and that the Holy Spirit has power over the enemy to save them. If we believe in the power of the blood, why should we not believe that the Holy Spirit will convict them, and that Jesus will save their soul at His appointed time?

Welcome Home My Child

Christ's Kingdom is all about home-coming celebration. This is why Jesus included the stories about the lost being found. The Shepard left the ninety and nine to rescue the one sheep that had strayed away and was found. We must keep in mind it was a sheep and not a goat that was lost. The stories that Jesus told about lost things are meant for our encouragement today, even though, the coin was lost it never lost its image or value and the prodigal son could hardly finish his confession to the father as a result of the fathers embrace and welcome home. We can only imagine the tears of Joy that flowed that day when the estranged son fell into the arms of a loving, forgiving father to wear His fathers ring.

God wants our confession for our sins, but He is always more interested in forgiving us, than to remind us of how we failed Him.

The story is told of a certain boy who also had become prodigal and left home after years of wondering. He had thoughts about his father and mother not knowing if they were still alive. One day, he decided to return to the old home place he remembered as a child, but decided to first write a letter asking if he would be accepted and welcomed. Since he would be taking the train that went by the old home place where he had played as a child he wrote in his letter, "If I'm welcomed to come home, please place a white sheet on the wash line so I will know that it's alright to get off the train.

Hours passed until the train finally neared the edge of town, the house would be just around the next bend. The young man could no longer stay in his seat, but stood outside the passenger car watching for the white sheet, to his excitement, there is was! Not just one sheet on the wash line, but white sheets were blowing in the breeze across the entire wash-line. The trees and shrubbery were all covered with white sheets and his parents were outside waving their arms with white sheets in their hands to say, "Welcome home son!" Welcome home is just another way of saying, "I forgive!"

The young man was overwhelmed with joy. Can you see the tears running down his face, can you identify with his uncontrollable emotions as he was embraced by his father and mother after all those years. Does this story communicate anything that you can identify with? If so, allow your tears to wash your soul."

Several years earlier, I had shared that story in a sermon I had presented in the presence of my parents. It was thanksgiving day and we always looked forward to travel the many miles back home to celebrate the event with a grand buffet that mother had prepared. As we turned into the long lane that led to the farm house, I suddenly noticed white sheets on the shrubbery and Dad and Mother were standing out in the yard waving white sheets to also welcome us home and to also say, "We forgive!"

Just in case you have an estranged relationship with a wayward child, never forget to pray with unconditional forgiving love. Remember the white flag of welcome. If you are a prodigal take that ride home and receive the white flag of welcome and surrender to the love it represents. But most of all think of the Pearly White City and streets of pure gold and the welcome that awaits the redeemed souls that trusted the Lord for their salvation. Sons and daughters who have decided to come home trusting the Lord for their welcomed acceptance, don't be afraid; Jesus will receive you just as you are. Don't miss the moment when He wipes away our tears and His welcome home Words, *"Well done, good and faithful servant, enter into the joy of your Lord!"* White flags on earth represent the heavenly hosts in heaven dressed in white to welcome every sinner home.

You Have Two Choices

Dad's letters would arrive at our Mountain City, Tennessee mailbox every week; he delighted to share his stories. "Son, do you want a good illustration for your Sunday sermon was not unusual?" In one of his letters he shared with me how that a group of Amish families had moved to the western part of the State and apparently were not welcomed by the community, including the town folks, as well as the local banker who expressed rejection by not accommodating the farmers with needed cash.

One of these farmers became aware that while they attended Sunday church service someone was helping themselves to their gas they used to operate the milking machine. Deciding to stay at home while the family went to church, the farmer would stay in the barn to see who their visitor might be. It wasn't long after his wife and children left that a car pulled up to the gas tank, the man got out of his car and in his trunk were two large gas cans. He proceeded to fill the one and as the farmer approached from behind, the man was startled and attempted to leave, "Wait a minute," said the farmer, "you didn't fill the other can, you came for gas and we need to fill the other can." Still the man tried to leave until the farmer said, "Sir! You have two choices, either we fill all the cans or I will report you to the police!" They filled the cans. Again the man attempted to leave until the farmer said, "My wife and children are coming home soon and we want you to be our Sunday dinner guest. My wife will prepare a good meal for you and we can get better acquainted." Again the man attempted to leave, until the farmer again said, "My friend you have two choices, have lunch with us or I will report you to the authorities."

Can you even begin to imagine how that man felt with those little eyes staring at him as he tried to swallow his food? The conversation wasn't too exciting Dad said, and than when the man got up from the table the farmer said, "Now next Sunday we don't have church service, so we want you to bring your family, we want to meet them also and again be our dinner guests." The man responded by saying, "I suppose I have two choices."

The moral of this story is what happened as a result of all this. News spread around the community and the local town folks. When the Banker heard what happened, the farmers were invited to come and borrow all the money they needed, the man and his family became the best of friends with the Amish farm families, and the Amish farmer practiced forgiveness in a Jesus kind of way. "Good story Dad!" I can't wait for more, it makes for good preaching!"

Might there be someone in your life that you need to forgive, by doing so, you will not only set them free, you will set yourself free, and establish renewed friendships.

Be Careful How You Say Goodbye!

My Father had a long battle with cancer in his larynx. He had lost his beautiful tenor voice and the ability to talk other than with a vibrator. I was preparing for my next message and was in need for a good illustration. For no other reason than to honor my Father, I decided to call him and ask for his permission to use something I remembered from my childhood for a sermon I was preparing.

Every year the New Holland Sales Stables held their annual all day horse sale. People gathered from far and near for the event, farmers would talk about the things of interest and since I was just a young boy I soon became bored and looked for things to entertain myself and pass the time. I noticed a poor old man sitting on an old tree stump with a severe leg injury. His pant leg was rolled up exposing what appeared to be painful sores. I became drawn into his situation since I was interested in seeing how many people would respond to his appeal for money as he held out his cup as they walked by.

My real question was, "what will my Father do should he happen to see the man". I had already decided that I would make him aware of the man should he still be there when we leave to do the evening farm chores.

Hours passed even though many people stared at the man. Not one person gave him any money, and I was greatly disturbed. Just then, I saw Dad coming, "What will he do I wondered?" He walked right past the man and never saw him, I thought. He stopped abruptly and looking back pulled his wallet from his pocket. I witnessed my awesome Daddy emptying all the bills from his wallet into that mans cup and without a word spoken he took my hand and off we went.

I looked back at the old man who was in awe. His mouth opened in surprise; Dad never mentioned what took place that day, but I remembered it well.

Now years had gone by and Dad was getting weaker and we all realized that he might soon be leaving us. I simply wanted to honor him in this way, he had released me to follow my call in life and I was grateful for the relationship we now enjoyed together. Not one week went by in all those years that we served the congregation in Tennessee that he failed to write me a letter telling about life on the farm and about the people who would come to visit. It wasn't unusual for prominent people finding their way to the farm including Lord Snowdon from London who wrote a story about Dad and Mother for McCall's Magazine with their photo as the center fold.

"Please make a recording and send it to me," Dad said. But I couldn't, my Daddy died soon after that conversation. Mother had just stepped into another room for just a moment following their breakfast; when she returned Dad had passed away still sitting at the table, in front of him was his open Bible from where he had been reading.

Eye Witnesses to Heaven

Heaven is not a myth, it is very real. The Bible provides hundreds of references to Heaven. Old Testament saints saw the City of God afar off by faith and through God's promise and by their visions and revelations.

Not until the apostle John was cast on the Isle of Patmos did we have a fuller revelation and description of the beautiful City of God. History records that John spent around eighteen months on Patmos, even though he had been placed in a vat of oil; God spared his life for this great revelation so that we might realize what is prepared for our eternity.

There have been many eye witnesses to the reality of heaven, numerous individuals with near death experiences testify to the beauty of heaven, how they went through the valley of the shadow of death, how they heard music as never before with awesome sights never imagined, how they felt love as never before even being introduced to loved ones that had passed away many years ago. Some have testified of having seen their babies that passed away, of being introduced to Old Testament saints.

One pastor shared his story with me of how he had lived a rebellious life while serving in the armed forces, how he fell in love with a Jewish girl and discovered her parents disapproval of their marriage since he was a Gentile. When this was discovered, they decided she would become pregnant, thinking the girls parents would approve; they didn't, so they decided to abort the child. Following the abortion everything changed, their love for each other grew cold and they separated.

Now the young man decided to move to another part of the country. It was here that someone introduced him to Jesus Christ; he accepted and soon enrolled in seminary to study to become a pastor. Upon his first assignment he said, "Every time I stood in the pulpit to preach, words failed me, all I could think of was the child we had aborted. After serving several congregations it was always the same, words would fail me and I felt condemned and could not find forgiveness. I resigned as pastor and decided to fast and pray until I found peace of mind. For days I fasted doing nothing but pray. One day as I was praying, I went into a trance and had a vision. I was taken by the hand of an angel who took me to heaven saying," I must introduce you to someone." Sixteen years had gone by since we had aborted our child, the angel said, "I want you to meet someone who loves you," I saw the most beautiful sights I had ever seen, the music was beyond description, then a young boy appeared and extended his hand in welcome and said, "Hello Dad, its alright, I'm so happy here!" The man said, "The vision left me and an overwhelming peace came upon me and my life was changed forever." He went on again to become a pastor and has served in various capacities in church leadership.

I Saw the Face of Jesus

It was a nice spring day and I was preparing to leave for a revival service in another state when I received the call to come to our local hospital immediately, this was not unusual for me as a pastor having been there many times before.

A certain lady that we had known for a number of years had been struggling with cancer and had been admitted to the hospital. That night she became very weak, three doctors were called to her room and every attempt was made to save her life to no avail.

The local funeral director was notified by the doctors to remove the body; they had signed the death certificate and were together leaving the room. As they walked down the hallway they heard singing coming from the room they had just left. As they entered the room, to their surprise, the woman was sitting up in her bed singing, "I saw the face of Jesus."

As I walked into her room she said, "David I saw the face of Jesus. I want you to tell my story and since you have a radio broadcast, I will be able to tell many people about heaven and to prepare for the time they too will leave this world.

"For the past several days I was not feeling well and I asked the Lord if there was anything I could do for Him, I love singing in the choir, but I felt as if I had an unfinished task for the Lord, so I prayed, "Lord use me in any way that will honor you, I am willing to do anything."

All I remember is, I went through a dark tunnel but I was not afraid, it was so peaceful, then I saw light in the distance and heard beautiful music. I remember coming out of the tunnel but I was not afraid, everything was so bright and the colors were so different. Then a figure appeared. I could never see His face, but His voice sounded like running water, and as He turned His head He said, "Don't come any closer;

I want you to go back and get your daughter." His voice had strength that just made me want to praise Him. I saw family members that had died long ago, I saw beautiful gates, the entrance was so brilliant and Jesus was walking with me. I asked Jesus if I could sing in the choir, all the while I felt like I was floating, my body felt so different from what I knew it to be, I heard music and the most beautiful singing I had ever heard, I felt so pure and clean."

"When can I come back?" she asked, Jesus said, "Three or four," David what did He mean by three or four?" The ladies' daughter was not a Christian, neither were the doctors. "I felt myself going back through the tunnel but this time it was different, there were people helping me, then I woke up and I was singing, "I saw the face of Jesus," and I was chanting Psalm (148-150), I did not remember these verses, could we read them together.

The room was filled with a presence I had never felt. What an experience to leave for a week of revival meetings. During the next several months the daughter accepted Christ as her Savior. The three doctors were saved and some of the nurses, a revival spread throughout our area and her story has been shared around the world, three months after all this happened she passed away.

Have a Good Flight

Ben and Marlene were in their senior years. We had never met them until we saw them holding hands as they strolled through the market place. It was obvious that they were not only in their senior years, but they were very much in love. We had always been drawn to the market place. It seemed like the environment Jesus would want to be to meet the people as they were. My comment to them was, "You two must be in love!" Their immediate response was, "We just got married!" As they shared with us how they had discovered each other their story became even more interesting. Ben had worked for a laundry firm in Virginia and Marlene worked for a laundry supplier in Atlanta, Georgia. Every week for forty years Ben and Marlene would converse on the phone as Ben would place his order for supplies. Now Ben's wife suddenly passed away; soon after that Marlene's husband also died, Ben said, "I decided that the two of us should meet after all these years having never met other than our phone conversations. Ben traveled to Atlanta and it was love at first sight.

Several years following our acquaintance, Ben suddenly became ill. When we received the call from Marlene telling us that Ben might not make it, I asked Marlene if they had a second phone so that we could have prayer together, as we prayed we simply asked for the Lord's will to be done and prayed that if it would be His will that Ben's life would be spared so they could still enjoy their life together. It was a very simple faith prayer trusting the Lord for a miracle healing. Several days following our prayer conversation the phone rang and I did not recognize the voice, "I'm Ben!" the voice said, "you called and prayed with me the other day, I'm calling to tell you I'm fine, something happened to me and I feel really good!"

Three years had gone by when we again received a call but this time it was Ben's sister who also lived in our area telling us that if we want to see Ben we would have to do that today, that this time he would not survive. Having been traveling through our area Ben was admitted to our local hospital. Ben greeted us with his usual smile and again we prayed and laughed together.

"Ben, I must tell you about the time when my granddad left this world. My two aunts were in the hospital room with him as he described the sights he was seeing, and then there was the sound of wings flying through the closed window and granddad went to heaven, so Ben! "Have a good flight!"

The family picked up on that comment and shared it with their friends including the pastor that was asked to conduct the funeral service. Not realizing that one simple comment would have such an effect and that by that comment I was asked to conduct the funeral service. The old Baptist pastor said, "I want you to take as much time as you need, there will be many people here that never heard the gospel story, they need to hear about, "Have a good flight!"

Following my message which was short and to the point, the old Baptist preacher walked up to the podium and with his soft spoken voice shared the gospel of Jesus Christ for nearly an hour, still talking about our final flight into eternity and in that funeral parlor He said, "If you are here today and you are not ready to take your flight, I invite you to come to Jesus and receive Him as your personal Savior." Four people responded to that invitation.

Even in death granddad's life impacted the Kingdom of God. There is a day appointed when every one will take their flight into eternity. Jesus has done all that needs to be done for the salvation of our soul, He said, *"It is finished!"* Nothing can be added but our simple childlike faith to trust Him with our soul by asking Him to come into our heart and life, to repent from our sins, and to live in His righteousness by His grace.

The salvation experience can take place anywhere. As a pastor, I have seen many people coming to the altar in their surrender to Christ. I have also witnessed individuals coming to Christ in my art shop, in the public market place, anywhere, anytime; it takes about thirty seconds of our time to make our decision to receive Jesus Christ as our Savior and a life time to live it out. I personally know of individuals who were too busy with life and the stuff they hoped to acquire and things they chose to do that had absolutely no eternal value, things of this world. According to the way they died, and by the comments they made as they were dying, they did not go into eternal peace and rest.

Eternity is too long to be wrong, take this moment in time and think about it; at the end of this book you will find a helpful prayer and scripture to assist you in making your decision to receive Christ or to rededicate your life to Christ. Don't neglect the most valued part of your being, the soul will never die, it lives on forever either in the presence of the Lord or in the company of the lost. "Have a good flight!"

Chapter Five

God's Mercy Multiplied

Today is a brand new day, resurrection power is expressing itself as nature celebrates the newness of the day, the birds sing their morning song, and there has never been a morning like this since the dawn of creation. The same sunrise and sunset is never repeated, yesterday is past no matter how cruel or kind it may have been and tomorrow never really comes even though we anticipate our future. We make plans and prepare since we know we are an eternal creation in Christ and may leave this world before we take our next breath without a moments notice.

The unbeliever does not live with this same perspective concerning their eternity. In a sense they too live for the moment, but with different values about most everything, many living in the regret of their past to never prepare for their future eternity, knowing absolutely nothing about God's peace within their heart or the beauty of God's presence in worship.

"I will worship You toward Your holy temple, and praise Your name for Your loving kindness and Your truth; For You have magnified Your Word above Your

*name. In the day when I cried out, You answered me,
and made me bold with strength in my soul,"*

(Psalm 138:2-3).

*"And the peace of God, which surpasses all under-
standing, will guard your Heart and mind through
Jesus Christ,"*

(Philippians 4:7).

To experience God's peace in this present world makes us aware that our life in Christ does not reach its completion here; it is just the beginning of eternal transformations that we can only grasp by faith. God's peace and love for us, is as big as God Himself; His greatest desire is to make His presence real in the heart of every individual on this earth and in every generation.

This is why He sent His Son Jesus into the world to offer His peace to mankind as the *"Prince of Peace."* When Jesus was born in Bethlehem, the angels proclaimed, *"Glory to God in the highest, and on earth peace, goodwill toward man!"* (Luke 2:14).

Jesus fulfilled His mission to earth by bringing God's peace to mankind, making it available to *"whosoever will"*. Jesus ascended back to heaven to be seated at His Father's right hand interceding for the people on earth. But the best news of all is—- He is coming again to receive us out of this sinful world of unrest and uncertainty to receive us unto Himself, to share heaven with us forever, to enjoy and participate in His eternal peace and joy in a world without end!

The first time Jesus came as a baby, the next time He is coming on clouds of glory to catch-up His bride the Church. Those of us who have accepted Him as our personal Savior will be ushered into His prepared heaven with exceeding great joy to be with Him in a world without end.

Following that event many other events will unfold, including seven years of tribulation on the earth under the rule of the Antichrist system, followed by the Battle of Armageddon. The redeemed of God will witness the formation of the new earth and the holy city coming down from God out of heaven. Enoch, the seventh from Adam prophesied saying.

"Behold He comes with ten thousands of His saints to execute judgment on all, to convict all who are ungodly among them of all their ungodly deeds which they have committed in an ungodly way, and of all the harsh things which ungodly sinners have spoken against Him,"

(Jude 14:15).

According to John's revelation, Jesus rides out of heaven on a White Horse with the armies of heaven to destroy all the works of wickedness, including the devil himself; casting him into the bottomless pit. Jesus will bring to this present earth a thousand years of peace; and the redeemed will reign with Him.

"He shall judge between the nations, and rebuke many people; they shall beat their swords into plowshares, and their spears into pruning hooks; Nation shall not lift up sword against nation, neither shall they learn war anymore,"

(Isaiah 2:4-5).

The feet of Jesus will again one day stand on the Mount of Olives. He will enter the Eastern Gate through which He rode the donkey on the Day of Passover to set up His earthly Kingdom, and we will reign with Him forever and ever. The prophet Zechariah saw into the future when all this would come to pass and he said.

"And in that day His feet will stand on the Mount of Olives, which faces Jerusalem on the east and the Mount of Olives shall be split in two, from the east to west, making a very large valley; half of the mountain shall move toward the north and half of it to the south,"

(Zechariah 14:4).

God is Light and God is Love

Concerning His nature, God is light and God is love, as the creator He is the only source and sustainer of Life, the only one who can provide eternal life through His Son Jesus Christ. He offers not only eternal life, but enables us to live in this world victorious over the enemy of our soul. There is no peace in the absence of light. Disturbed peace produces turmoil and *"If we have hope in this life only we are of all men most miserable."*

Jesus Christ is the door into God's peace. If we knock the door will open; it is not a revolving door, nether is it automatic, it will only open as we knock or as we hear Jesus knocking on our hearts door, when we knock He will open that door that leads to life eternal.

"Ask and it will be given to you; seek, and you will find; knock and it will be opened"

(Matthew 7:7).

"Behold I stand at the door and knock, If anyone hears My voice and opens the door, I will come in to him and dine with him, and be with him,"

(Revelation 3:20).

God has an inexhaustible supply of everything we need to make it through this life if we choose to live out of His riches. Why then should we even become disturbed when the world around us seems to be in turmoil or fear and worry concerning the times in which we are living, especially when we claim to not identify with the world as citizens of God's Kingdom?

God informs us that we are not of this world that our citizenship is in heaven. He takes care of the lilies of the field and feeds every sparrow reminding us that we are more than many sparrows.

"Therefore I say to you, do not worry about your life, what you will eat or what you will drink; nor about your body, what you will put on. Is not life more than food and the body more than clothing?" look at the birds of the air, for they neither sow nor reap nor gather into barns; yet your heavenly Father feeds them. Are you not of more value than they?"

(Matthew 6:25-26).

Peace with God is a gift and also an acquired virtue by our acceptance that we have to access to receive. God's peace has to be accepted and appropriated before it can be experienced; faith is also a gift from God that has to be exercised. However, for all this to work, it must be acquired by having faith in God, for our right now need. His promise is,

95

"And my God shall supply all your need according to His riches in glory by Christ Jesus,"

(Philippians 4:19).

The Old Testament especially is a commentary of a people who learned to live by faith which developed by trusting God. "Now" faith always relies and depends upon that which we cannot see yet we believe, because "Now" faith has substance, we believe God who is able to do exceedingly abundantly above all we ask of Him and is beyond our capacity to think or imagine.

"Now faith is the substance of things hoped for, the evidence of things not seen,"

(Hebrews 11:1).

To illustrate the importance of action faith or a belief system that puts faith into action the following story applies very well. A man preparing to walk on a rope across Niagara Falls asked the onlookers if they believed that he could do it, they all jeered their approval. On his return walk, he asked the crowd again if they believed that he could accomplish his walk blindfolded, again they all jeered their approval, the third time he asked the crowd, "Do you believe that I can walk across this rope blindfolded carrying a man on my back," again the crowd jeered with their approval, but when he asked for a volunteer the crowd became silent.

The moral of the story is, its not difficult to believe about God, even the devil believes and trembles, but to believe with faith that all things are possible to them that believe, that with God nothing is impossible, and that God wants to bring His supernatural ability into our natural inability, transforming us into His image and likeness to live our lives by His power as He carries us through life and into eternity.

Allow the Lord to Fight your Battles

Faith and trust to receive God's peace that passes all understanding serves as a unity of purpose against the forces of evil that we encounter in this life. If we allow the battle to be the Lord's battle, we can relax, there are always more on our side then on the enemy's side because God and heaven are on our side, and we believe God! *"And if God is for us, who can be against us."*

Although we cannot fully understand God, we can still know and experience Him in our heart as well as our mind and soul. We know Him in our spirit through a personal relationship of faith in Jesus Christ and through the study of His Word and what the Bible teaches about His nature. God may also be described in terms of attributes; an attribute is an inherent characteristic of a person or being.

While we cannot describe God in a comprehensive way, we can learn about Him by examining His attributes as revealed in the Bible. The greatest revelation of God comes to us through the Bible, the inspired written record; both the existence of God and the nature of God are revealed in and through Jesus Christ.... Jesus stated, *"He that has seen me, has seen the Father"* (John 14:9).

God wants us to experience not only His gift of eternal life, but also His sustaining grace, not only to keep us from falling or from missing the mark, but to experience the highest level of relationship for time and eternity while we live on earth. He wants us to experience His power and peace to be completely intimate with Him. Without the peace of God in our heart, we have absolutely no spiritual power no matter what we profess to be and we become vulnerable to defeat and deception.

Even though we are covered and sheltered by the blood of Jesus, we can experience the turbulence of the enemy's wicked ways. The enemy works anyway he can to bring about our discouragement and destruction. He works through events and circumstances and through individuals and we have all been targets of his schemes.

Every child of God will agree that there is absolutely nothing bigger than God Himself! That everything created including all earthly powers, authorities, any adversity or principality known or unknown are all in subjection to God. He is **LORD Jehovah,** supreme in all power and authority, our present help in time of trouble.

God desires to saturate us with Himself

The Holy Spirit is in the world today to *"convict the world of sin, judgment and righteousness"*. Righteousness is all about experiencing God's peace in us, over us, and through us. We will never be in right standing before God apart from His peace in our heart and mind. Even though we may experience God's peace to the fullest measure, we can't explain or understand it because it is bigger than any human intellect, bigger than the universe and higher than the heavens, yet God is gracious and loving enough to live within our heart.

> *"That your hearts may be encouraged, being knit together in love, and attaining to all the riches of the full assurance of understanding, to the knowledge and mystery of God, both of the Father and of Christ, in whom are hidden all the treasures of wisdom and knowledge,"*

(Colossians 2:2-3).

Many individuals live with an intellectual knowledge concerning God without a heart-knowing experience. To know God with our heart we must have a born again experience to have a personal relationship with God through Jesus Christ and to discover *"the unsearchable riches in Christ"*.

The adversary of our soul robs many individuals from having peace with God. If we do not experience God's peace as a Christian, it becomes our responsibility to identify the sources that rob us from experiencing this peace. This means we might have to break friendships, it may mean confession for sin including a spirit of unforgiveness.

God desires that we understand His peace through a personal relationship. He will do everything necessary to make sure that we are both guarded and protected and that His peace possess' us through and through.

> *"...let the peace of God rule in your hearts, to which you were called in one body; and be thankful. Let the Word of Christ dwell in you richly in all wisdom, teaching and admonishing one another in psalms and hymns and spiritual songs, singing with grace in your hearts to the Lord. And whatever you do in word or deed, do all in the name of the Lord Jesus, giving thanks to God the Father through Him,"*

Colossians 3:14-17).

Even though all born again individuals become a part of the body of Christ, God always brings people into our lives that compliment us for who we are, comrades of the faith to make us strong in faith.

Do you ever wonder why it is that God allows certain people to become a part of your inner circle of friends, people that you think of as being cool! They fit your personality and compliment your life-style, they are your friends; even

Jesus had His inner circle of close friends. He never rejected anyone, but there were individuals that Jesus did not hang around with, if you study the Bible you will soon discover this truth about the life of Jesus and how He conducted Himself among humanity. Jesus was and still is a friend of sinners, the religious and self righteous crowd He avoided as much as possible, He even drove money changers out of the temple with a whip He had made Himself, but His word always was and still is, *"Whosoever will, may come."*

We must guard our peace and be selective as to who we associate with or who we allow to pray with us or over us. Be very careful who touches your life, both physically or spiritually, there must always be a unity of purpose for the Lord to bless our lives, negative people will spiral us down into the pit faster that anything on earth, they can cast a spirit of heaviness on us before we know what happened. We have been delivered from the power of darkness, so why should we even want to associate with darkness or negative people?

"He has delivered us from the power of darkness and conveyed us into the Kingdom of the Son of His love,"

(Colossians 1:13)

The Bible provides us with many interesting examples for our learning including a story in the Old Testament that has great signifience to being careful who we share our pearls with.

King Hezekiah was sick and strangers from a far country came to visit him. The King showed these strangers all his treasures of silver, gold, spices, ointment. He withheld nothing from these men he had never met. *"There was nothing in his house nor his dominion that King Hezekiah*

100

did not show them" (v.2). In an unexpected moment these strangers returned and carried away everything that King Hezekiah had in his possession including several of his sons. (Isaiah 39).

Cast Your Care upon the Lord

The Bible instructs us *"to bear one another's burdens,"* to weep with those who weep, to feel the hurt of the hurting, to care for the broken hearted and the dying, rightly interpreted this simply means to have empathy toward or with them to encourage them, but to bear or carry their burdens to Jesus, what can we do with someone's else's burdens unless we minister into someone's need in the name of Jesus? Absolutely nothing but to carry those burdens ourselves, we were not designed or created to do that and we would be robbing individuals of their greatest blessing and breakthrough to discover Jesus Christ in a new way in the midst's of their struggle and pain, the Bible plainly instructs us to cast our burdens upon Him.

"Casting all your care upon Him, for He cares for you,"

(1 Peter 5:7).

While attending seminary one of my assigned projects was to discover someone that I could challenge with the gospel becoming a spiritual significant other, a spiritual trusted friend to some other person. My project took me to Woodrow Wilson Rehabilitation Center in Virginia; It wasn't long until I discovered a young man in a wheel chair that I became drawn to. His name was John, he told me he was from East Tennessee, when I told him I had served as a pastor in that area his face lit up. "How did you receive your injuries?" I asked. Somewhat reserved, John told me how he played football for a major team and during a major event he was injured by another player. John was paralyzed from the waste down and had also sustained severe head injuries with a speech impediment.

I met with John once a week for several hours that entire summer and for the most part took him for a stroll in his wheel chair around the campus. "Tell me about your family?" I asked. Now John begins to cry weeping uncontrollably, "I really loved her; she was so beautiful, we were so in love! Now I lost her, even my parents or none of my former friends call me. I have lost my ability to be myself, but even worse than that, I lost all my friends, they never call me, not once have my parents even tried to contact me, I feel so alone!" What moved me more than anything was the fact that in all his loss, John didn't realize that his soul was also apparently lost.

A spiritual dynamic is now coming into play; we can never help anyone not even try to bear their burdens or bear them to Jesus until we have won their trust. Once we have won trust, we can do just about anything to move people beyond their situation introducing them to Christ.

As days and weeks went by John and I became very good soul friends, I was experiencing something of John's soul and John experienced my soul and we became soul-mates.

I shared with John some of my disappointments in life even with people that were close to me, but most of all, how I had discovered this wonderful best friend called Jesus. John listened intently to every word and at the proper moment I asked John if he would like to know my friend. He accepted the invitation and became a born again Christian.

My breakthrough moment came when we were strolling around the campus on a nice sunny day, there were no words spoken, the sky above was clear cerulean blue and John kept looking skyward. The silence was interrupted when John in an exuberant voice looked up and said, "Dave isn't God good!" I used those words for the title of my term paper.

John continued to grow in his new found faith in Christ, that's more then twenty years ago. I have no idea what ever became of John, but my life was also changed, it always is when we become an extension of who Jesus is in our world today, when we encounter individuals in His name and we become a spiritual significant other in a persons life.

There are many people like John in our world that need someone like you and me to bring a message of hope and peace into their disturbed lives. It is only as we become sensitive to their need, and as we open our heart to the Lord to be led by the Holy Spirit that these blessings will happen since we were all created in the image of God, allowing Him to become the solution through our compassion for humanities hurt and pain, allowing Jesus Christ to bring restoration and healing.

Protect Your Friendships

The enemy is a destroyer of peace and takes great delight by driving a wedge between those we love the most; it happens all the time, between spouses, parent child relationships, neighbors or friends, the list goes on. If you are not aware of this, choose to become a counselor and you will soon discover the devils mission field and his divisive tactics in coming between relationships to destroy them. Or dare to become all you can be for Christ and His Kingdom work and your so called friends will soon separate themselves from you and you will discover who your real soul-mate prayer-partner friends are. In reality most of the people we consider friends are only acquaintances.

We all know how it hurts to lose someone we had enjoyed sharing our life with, our peace can be shattered in a moment through various circumstances and the peace we enjoyed can be frustrated by fear, uncertainty or insecurity, we all have lost some very beautiful friends all because of misunderstandings.

Never listen or receive second-handed information, be pro-active, when in doubt do your own spiritual investigation of a situation or circumstances. The enemy will do everything in his power to rob us of God's peace within us; he will use circumstances, friends, family, financial situations, anything that becomes a distraction that works for him to make us miserable, insecure and lukewarm attempting to rob us of our personal peace with God.

We must Guard our Spirituality

The Psalmist wrote, *"My soul melts with heaviness; Strengthen me with Your Word"* (Psalm 119: 28).

The quickest way to acquire a spirit of heaviness is to live apart from God's Word, to allow the burdens of other people to weigh upon us not releasing them to Jesus, to live with self pity and to not feed upon God's Word believing Him for what He says as truth.

The spirit of heaviness originates out of our human nature, it may also be a fiery dart from the enemy, darts from the enemy are as spirits that afflict us to destroy us, we must always be aware of the enemy's strategy against us, we have an obligation to our own spiritual well being to denounce anything and everything that would jeopardize our peace with God. We must discern the difference between the spirit of heaviness which comes from our human spirit and the spirit of conviction which always comes from the Holy Spirit.

As born again believers, we have delegated authority to in the name of Jesus denounce anything that hinders us; we have the authority to call anything we desire into being; things that are not as if they already were right in our hand.

Anxiety is not from God, anxiety and fear come forth out of our carnal nature and our inability to fight off the fiery darts of the wicked one. We all have to fight the enemies of our soul; our flesh man reacts or responds to the forces of evil around us which are always caused by the god of this world through circumstances or situations we are facing. The enemy of our soul is an evil spirit, anxiety and fear, the spirit of heaviness and a host of other spirits are included in the enemy's arsenal to fight against us.

> *"Greater is He that is in us than he that is in the world. God has not given us the spirit of fear, but of power, [God power] and of love and of a sound mind,"*

> (Timothy 1:7).

The Bible warns that fear is not only a tormenting foe, but fear also robs us of our inner happiness and peace of mind. Inner happiness is not possible for the persons that are occupied with self. Inner happiness is based on knowing Jesus Christ personally and knowing in our heart that He is everything He claims to be for us, in us, and through us. Inner happiness is the joy of living where every provision for physical emotional and spiritual well-being is provided by our [Abba Daddy] heavenly Father.

Chapter Six

Forgiveness,
The Music of the Soul

The entire Bible is a message of redemption and forgiveness; it is God's story of love for His own creation that became deceived by satan. Through the ages, God has raised up prophets, preachers, teachers and evangelists to declare His message of redemption to the people. Mighty men and women of God have been brought to the frontlines of spiritual warfare by the Holy Spirit to declare the message of grace that is greater than all our sin. God wants every individual to understand and experience His redeeming love and grace through Jesus Christ; this is why He spoke to men like the prophet Isaiah who declared,

> *"Come now, and let us reason together," Says the Lord, Though your sins are like scarlet, they shall be white as snow; though they are red like crimson, they shall be as wool,"*

(Isaiah 1:18).

Before we can experience God's peace in our soul, we have to first receive His forgiveness according to the riches of His grace and His kindness toward us as sinners. As forgiven, we have an eternal inheritance; God's peace in us becomes our greatest treasure as we live in this present life. The treasures of this world can never be compared to the treasures of the Kingdom of God. God's peace is the greatest treasure we could ever discover, it is like digging for gold and finding a rich vein, the deeper we dig the richer it becomes. God's peace can never be compared to anything this world offers. Peace is a word which provides several different meanings; in the Old Testament it meant completeness, soundness, and the well being of a total person. Peace for the individual simply means, all is well with our soul.

"You will keep him in perfect peace, whose mind is stayed [fixed] on you, because he trusts in you,"

(Isaiah 26:3).

Agony is the opposite of peace and is defined as extreme pain, mental anguish, distress, excruciating soul pain. I have witnessed individuals leaving this world with the agony of soul pain, the deep regret for having rejected Christ as their personal Savior to face the consequences of their rejection, eternal separation from God.

The peace that Jesus provides is different from any other peace, it is more than just a happy state of mind, or temperament, it is deeper, stronger and eternal and the only thing that we cherished in life that will stay with us as we enter heaven. It is attained through the victory of the cross and was birthed out of extreme excruciating soul, Spirit and body pain by Jesus, to provide peace for our souls and our eternity with Him in glory.

God's peace through Jesus Christ goes deeper than our intellect or our passion; it is a positive spiritual endowment, as a gift from God that will continue with us in our spirit forever. Sickness cannot destroy it, poverty cannot rob it and bereavement only makes it more real, and if we are born again, the approach of death even more peaceful. The world which cannot give it cannot take it away, its roots are in the immovable assurance of God's amazing grace and divine acceptance and favor through the blood of Jesus Christ.

If we should lose our peace through whatever circumstances, we have an advocate Jesus Christ, our personal friend and God as our heavenly Father, who always works in harmony with the Holy Spirit for our spiritual well being, to restore that which became lost. God's Word to us is He would never leave us or forsake us, that He is always with us to comfort, guide and keep us from falling. And if we fall, Jesus always restores what becomes lost by our confession, whatever mess we make out of our lives; He will make it right through the blood of the cross. If we sin, we have an advocate which simply means Jesus is our friend to help us in our time of need.

He brought peace of mind to the sinners of His day who became converted by His grace. He brought salvation to harlots and prostitutes and while the self righteous crowd rejected His offer of peace with their religious opposition and ridicule. His peace forged a path through the centuries of time and will continue through the age's over- coming every obstacle that stands in its way, and as long as time will last the *"Prince of Peace"* will turn our turmoil into tranquility. Jesus Christ has become man's strongest connection with God through the centuries and no matter what storms we encounter, Jesus is always the Master over the storm and we can appropriate His power to overcome every demon from hell.

The Enemy of Holiness

Once we receive and experience the peace of God by faith, it gradually spreads its roots over our entire spiritual being through the sanctifying power of the Holy Spirit; and the only thing in the world that can destroy it is sin.

The enemy's purpose is to steal our treasure, and our peace, to cripple our spiritual power, and contaminate our holiness. His purpose is to make us as miserable as he is himself; this is why he is justly referred to as our adversary. He is the enemy of holiness and of everything that is pure, right, and good, he tempts us to sin, he accuses us of wrong doing even when we are innocent, he studies our human nature and fits his plots and schemes, tempting us to failure. He understands lust nature, greed, our earthliness, or the greatest of all evils, pride. He understands the condemnation of pride since he lost his position in heaven as director of heavens choir and was cast out of heaven as a result of his pride.

The enemy of our soul is the author of evil, an adversary of truth, the corruption of the world, he is man's perpetual enemy; he plants snares, suggests thoughts, brings evil devises to pass, he sows discord, contention and disrupts peace; he delights to enter a family situation or a peaceful congregation of people to disrupt them. He lures men of God to lose their anointing by doing that which is sinful, unholy and forbidden by God.

When anxieties and fear control our lives, we are defeated and become pawns for the enemy, this becomes very dangerous ground. Anxiety always breeds bitterness, and bitterness paralyzes us spiritually. The only way back to God is to confess our sins, plead His blood, and receive His forgiveness. His arms are always opened to us to receive us back into full fellowship justified, "Just as if we had not sinned."

The Virtue of Peacemaking

How can we become Christ-like in our peacemaking efforts? With the experience of years of pastoral and counseling ministry, I have concluded that the measure and extent of one's spirituality and holiness is determined by our actions and attitude, and if the enemy robs us of our holiness, breakdown, surprise sin failure soon follows and we become robbed of our personal peace and all peace making efforts and everything can go wrong before we realize what happened.

How do we react when a fellow believer commits an immoral sin? Do we reject and condemn them, or do we love them into a restored forgiven relationship with Christ. In most cases, I have witnessed the worst of human nature, rather than working toward healing and restoration, I have witnessed critical rejection and unforgiveness and there can be absolutely no peace in ones heart or soul when our peace becomes lost by our unforgiving spirit. Paul admonished the believers to be careful how we process a fallen fellow believer by saying,

"Those of you who are spiritual, restore such a one in the spirit of meekness considering you might also have your surprise moment when you least expect it, and in a moment of temptation you too will fall.

(See Galatians 6:1-20 Paraphrased).

Sins of surprise are the sins which Paul commends to the care of Christians friends, it is usually the sins of surprise that overtake the unexpected victim of the enemy.

The person who took their first drink in a weak moment had no intention of becoming an alcoholic. The person who smoked their first marijuana had no plans of becoming a drug addict. The person who had a weak immoral moment had no intention to ever commit adultery. The person who explored the internet for the first time had no intention of becoming addicted to pornography. The person in a fit of anger had no intention to commit murder.

The enemy always magnifies our missteps and surprise immoral sins or failures making them much more severe and almost irreparable, because of all the people who become hurt in the downfall. Paul is admonishing us as believers to not be quick in passing judgment lest we also be tempted with the same sin and surprise failure. We must also realize that Jesus came not for the righteous, He came to call sinners to repentance, to pick up the fallen, to care for those who are struggling to keep the faith, to carry those who are unable to walk on their own, He came for the rejects of society!

As Spirit filled Christians we have the ability to discern the difference between right and wrong, between good and evil. We can discern what is of God and what is of the god of this world. No anxiety, displeasure, grief, or sorrow can overtake a surrendered heart; we may become overwhelmed for the moment until the grace of God reveals itself as sufficient for our need to again experience the joy of the Lord as our strength. Because we will know what to do with conflict, we release it all to Jesus and in turn He gives us the victory to overcome, and our heart-knowing faith will maintain our peace with God.

To be able to cast out vain imaginations we must *"know the truth, and the truth will set us free."* Vain imaginations can easily defeat us; this is why we must never entertain foolish negative thoughts. Only as we overflow with the life and love of Jesus Christ, out of our inner most being, are we able to live in total victory and it becomes an expression of our sanctification in process. When we personally discover who Jesus is for us and in us as earthen vessels and when the Holy Spirit controls our life the works of the flesh are replaced by the fruit of the Spirit.

If you are not experiencing this overflow, check your heart, and your attitude, sometimes there is a room in our heart that we don't even want to go because of what is hidden there, and we live in denial; it may be un-confessed sin or a harbored grudge, a spirit of un-forgiveness, we know its there but we are afraid to confront it.

Only Jesus can clean that room and when He does, He fills every room of our heart to overflowing with Himself so that there is no room for anything unholy. When we ignore those rooms we are ignorant of God's Word and His deliverance power for us. We do not heed the voice of the Holy Spirit convicting us that something is not right or we simply choose to live in our carnal nature rather than being committed to the Lordship of Christ.

Nothing can be more profound and persuasive than for the Lord God of heaven becoming our personal friend, keeping us safe and protected by our total surrender to His Lordship. When we are completely surrendered to Jesus Christ with a full dependence for His wisdom for us, we should have no problem in bringing all our cares, even secret sins to Him and to leave them there. He turns the cares of our life from thorns to roses, our valley experiences into mountain top victories and we will know without a doubt that God has complete control of our lives, since He is always working in us so that He might work through us for His glory and for our eternal well being.

> *"If God is for us, than who can be against us?" He that spared not His own Son but delivered Him up for us all, how shall He not with Him also freely give us all things."*

> *(Romans 8:32).*

The treasure of God's peace must be accepted by our simple faith in God's Word with a complete surrender, all hindering thoughts of doubt, the worries of life, including all financial, physical and spiritual concerns have to be placed at the foot of His cross.

Our first step into victory is to pray that Jesus would cast out any secret sins, any vain imaginations and fill that room with His Holy Spirit. We must appropriate His peace by praying audible prayer words; our silent passive meditation will not conquer our foe. We must speak audible prayer words into the atmosphere in the name of Jesus.

When our prayer words are inspired and anointed by the Holy Spirit they burst through the atmospheric heavens like a missile exploding in the face of the enemy. Our prayer words destroy the enemy's evil intent and ascend to God's throne as incense with a sweet smelling aroma.

Ashes always accompany smoke and smoke always rises, but ashes return to the ground. Just as our prayers ascend to heaven, the ashes as ambers, return setting many things ablaze. God returns our answered prayers as burning embers and He sets those areas ablaze with His grace, the refining fire of the Holy Spirit, the counsel of the wisdom of His Spirit as He battles against the enemy in behalf of our intercessory prayer words. It may be children living hundreds of miles away that suddenly become affected by our prayers.

Living in the Spirit of Freedom

A number of things happen when we experience God's peace. Everything seems to fall into place and life begins to make sense; it's really the only way to feel good about everything including ourselves.

It takes God's Holy Spirit in our heart to free our mind from distractions and the things of this world, to convict and correct us when we become distracted from our life with Him by becoming attracted to what this world offers.

We must daily remind ourselves that while we are in the world we are not of the world, our citizenship is in heaven, therefore, our affections must also be on things eternal, this world will in time pass away and the only thing that will matter when we take our flight into eternity are the things we did that honored the Lord, that served His Kingdom purposes on earth as in heaven.

We must stand firm on the solid Rock, Christ Jesus, who alone is our solid ground. We cannot fight on a quagmire, as soft ground or quick-sand. We will never stand firm by our own resolutions and purposes, only as we stand firm on the promise of His Word can we appropriate His promised victory to overcome the world. Our faith in the Lion of Judah delivers us from the roaring lion from the bottomless pit, our delivering Lion against the devouring lion; the greatness of His power becomes lived out in us, for us, by the indwelling presence of the Holy Spirit.

Do Not Become Distracted by the World

Our focus can easily become distracted by what is taking place in this world and we can become fearful because of the uncertainty of our future well being as we live out our lives on the earth. We have all rightfully invested in the things of this world as good stewards and we become attached to those things. It is who we are and what we do as human beings. God wants us to replenish, reproduce and be keepers of the earth to multiply, to labor and prosper for His glory, but not to loose sight of who He is and what He desires to do with His invested interest in us, we are on the earth for one purpose, that is to be Kingdom builders to lay up treasure in heaven.

We have all worked hard and have planned for our future well being, to be self- sufficient and independent especially in our senior years. So how do we respond when our future looks uncertain, when our retirement funds may no longer be there by the time we will need them?

Our first reaction should be to thank God for reminders. Every time God allows major events to take place in the world it always serves as a means to draw our attention to Him, to remind us that we are only visitors to this present world and that our real life awaits us in the world to come, that is—eternity with Him in glory.

We must always see our life from God's perspective, to realize that life at its best is as a vapor in time, compared to eternity, to better understand this we must focus on God's Word and realize that this present world system will some day pass away, that there is a whole new world order coming, a Kingdom that has no end and when we are confronted with difficult situations, we are not moved by events or circumstances, we are naturally moved to prayer since we are committed to the Lordship of Jesus Christ.

Praying for the Spirit of Discernment

Our philosophy and ideology concerning the things of this life including the interpretation of scripture is something that we have to come to understand with our heart as we are taught by the Holy Spirit.

If we only listen to what other people say, all we will ever know is what some other person said, and we will never know for ourselves what God said and that may sometimes be deceptive, misleading and ignorant on our part. Bible dictionaries, historical records, the history and culture of the people of the Bible are vitally important to understand the Bible, but only as the Holy Spirit opens the Word of God to us can we more fully comprehend what He is wanting us to receive and understand complimenting our faith in Him.

While serving as pastor for a small congregation in the foothills of the Great Smoky Mountains, I learned much about the culture of the people, there were a few who couldn't read the Bible so they went by what some other person said, One day an older lady asked me this question, "Preacher, doesn't the Bible say that if you cast your bread upon the water it will come back buttered." What the Bible really says is, *"in many days hence it will return."* The lady however captured the depth of the meaning of the Word.

We all agree that Jesus is coming soon, but we also realize that He may not come for a very long time. Our responsibility is to be prepared and ready for whenever He decides to rapture His body, the Church, into glory. Even though there will be signs of His coming that will happen without a moments notice and in the twinkling of an eye. This is why the Bible warns-

"Therefore you also be ready, for the Son of Man is coming at an hour you do not expect,"

(Matthew.24:44).

"Do not love the world or the things in the world. If anyone loves the world, the love of the Father is not in him. For all that is in the world - the lust of the flesh, the lust of the eye, and the pride of life - is not of the Father but is of the world. And the world is passing away, and the lust of it; but he who does the will of God abides forever,"

(1 John 2:17).

As Christians we are the most privileged and blessed people in the world. We have the greatest challenge in the history of humanity, we too, can communicate with God just as His people always have; however, we have an advantage over the Old Testament saints, they did not have delegated authority to pray in the name of Jesus as we do today. Our prayer words can bring about the greatest results, the greatest spiritual move of God ever. It is therefore time to pray and seek the Lord. We know by our faith that Jesus is the answer for our world, for His body the Church and for every individual person.

How can we unite our hearts to pray as never before? This is an important question that we must sooner or later answer because we have been commissioned by God to pray without ceasing. The answer is in our spoken prayer words, to meditate or to write our prayer is acceptable and God will honor and the Bible is proof of that, but think about your words from this perspective.

Our audible words become the most powerful means of communicating to one another and with God, once our words are spoken into the atmosphere not even God can recall them. If they are printed on paper they become a document, if they are harsh, negative miss-spoken words they can always be forgiven but never recalled.

To help us to understand the power of the spoken word try to imagine how your spouse would have reacted had you not verbalized your engagement, or when the preacher asked the question, will you take this woman to be your wedded wife? Suppose you would have meditated or thought your response without saying anything, what do you think would have happened? To say "I do" made your vow official before God, to your spouse, and those who witnessed your commitment.

This is why our audible public confession of faith, confessing Jesus Christ as our personal Savior is important to God. He honors our words of confession of faith in Him, including the confession of our sins, it is important that we verbalize our words in the name of Jesus. When we pray to our Father in heaven the Holy Spirit will convey our prayer words to God who sits on His Throne eagerly waiting to hear from His people, God seldom does anything apart from His people, this is why He gave us the authority to win the lost, to pray for the sick, to care for the dying and to cast out demons, or anything else He wants done in His name that becomes supernatural.

He knows our thoughts afar off and His Word affirms that even before we pray the answer is on the way, as important as our prayer words are we are not limited to just words, there are those times when we simply wait before Him since we are at a loss for words.

Jesus is seated at the right hand of the Father making intercession for us and our prayers are answered according to God's will. God's voice is communicated back to us through the Holy Spirit and Jesus said, *"My sheep know My voice"*.

The power of spoken words has become very real to Anna Mary and I, both of us recorded our voice on tape for many years, she conducted a children's story time program on our world-wide outreach. We preserved some of those tapes and they are as powerful today as they were forty years ago. I recorded my first crusade to the West Indies and the message is as clear today as it was then and if properly preserved will last into future generations long after we leave this world.

We all remember words that were spoken as far back as memory will take us. Some of those words were positive while others were negative; we cherish the positive and forget the negative. This is why God created us above the animal kingdom providing us with the ability to speak words. He desires our praise and worship and in a positive way communicates with His world.

One of our spiritual treasures is that of worship, *"the Lord inhabits the praises of His people."* Individuals who are suppressed with the cares of life find it difficult to worship and praise the Lord; it's difficult to sing and rejoice when we are despondent, upset in our spirit, sad or crying, complaining how bad life is. One of the purposes of God bringing us into this world was meant to be an instrument of worship. We were born to praise the Lord at all times, becoming instruments of righteousness for God's glory.

What has enabled me to work through difficult times was to listen to praise music while I work or drive, or when I can't sleep, even in my quiet time it is helpful to draw close into God's presence. The enemy takes his leave when we are praising the Lord, and the Lord inhabits the praises of His people, there is always victory in Jesus when we fill the places of our habitation with praise, supplication and thanksgiving.

I Will Praise You While I Live!

Love awakens love, *"We love Him because He first loved us."* Only as we live in the freedom that comes from a right relationship with the Lord are we able to praise Him out of a heart of love and with our whole heart. This is what makes living with the freedom to forgive every violation and annoyance that the enemy brings our way; for me forgiveness is the music of the soul that conditions our heart for the Holy Spirit to set us free indeed! As our Maestro, He lifts us into a realm of bliss and tranquility that provides us with a foretaste of heaven.

As we praise and worship Him for who He is, our thoughts about God and His will for us comes into focus and that causes everything to become foundational in all our relationships.

It is God's love in us that motivates us into everything we desire since it is a love that originates from Him and operates through us by His will and power, back and forth, reciprocating in and out, overflowing, saturating, reflecting and abounding, coming forth from Him to us only to return to Him.

As we praise Him for who we are in Him, out of a heart of gratitude for loving us, this motivates us, it inspires us, and it is God's own love shed abroad in our heart that sets our spirit ablaze with praise worship and thanksgiving.

Chapter Seven

Heart-Knowing Faith

When our heart is right with God all things become possible for us, we find ourselves living in the excitement of expectancy, our natural state of being will anticipate the supernatural presence and power of God in us, to enable us to do exceedingly abundantly above all we cannot do on our own since God made a promise to us and we know He is not a man that He should lie.

To understand the dynamic of God's presence and peace in our heart, we must understand our Adamic nature and how we acquire God's peace. Our natural mind is always in subjection to our spiritual heart. Our heart must first become aware of its fallen condition, the heart is referred to in scripture as a heart of flesh and can become rock-hard through rebellion; however, by the convicting power of the Holy Spirit our flesh heart can be transformed to take on the nature and personality of Jesus Christ in us, *"Christ in you, the hope of glory."*

The Adamic carnal mind has the potential for the most horrendous evil thought and action since it is under the control of the god of this world, satan. Not until our heart is surrendered to Jesus Christ can the new heart renew the old mind.

The unregenerate heart is *"desperately wicked,"* and controls the tongue and our mind, the tongue being, *"full of deadly poison,"* and may still express itself through our carnal nature after we become a born again Christian. Heart-knowing faith always happens as the mind is renewed, when our renewed mind and our new heart beat in rhythm with God's Word. The Holy Spirit will transfuse the peace of God that passes all understanding into our heart, this can happen in no other way, this is not reform, or turning over a new leaf, this is regeneration a work performed only by the Holy Spirit.

Only as God reveals Himself to our heart by the convicting power of the Holy Spirit, can our mind become transformed. When this takes place, we see life from God's perspective, our new heart renews our old mind and our mind attains spiritual knowledge as the new heart dictates information to the renewed mind.

Our mind thinks out of the intellectual part of who we are. As *"Born from above"* we are now capable to think faith thoughts, nothing impossible thoughts, and redemptive thoughts. The believer does not think as unbelievers think. Believers are justified by faith; therefore they walk and think by faith to become what we think, this is why we must always dwell on the good and not on that which is carnal or evil.

Becoming a Power Force for God

Our heart was created to be our life source, to maintain life, to be our life force as a human being, but God had much greater plans than that. His plan, purpose and will is to live in the heart of human beings, to reproduce Himself in the heart and life of men, women, boys and girls and for redeemed humanity to become an extension of who He is, to do through redeemed humanity what He always did with delegated authority. To provide human kind with His life in us while we live on earth, to give us His peace, to experience and revel in His love, to provide us with His protective care in every area of our life. This includes our physical, mental, and spiritual well being and above all eternal life through His Son Jesus Christ, to be a power force, *"to live and move and have our being in Him,"* "to be light to the world," a spiritual force as representatives of His Kingdom and a testimony of His grace in us for time and eternity.

While attending art school, I became aware of the right and left side of the human brain and how we function according to the dictates of one side or the other and how that will influence the picture we paint with our life. I also learned that there is a part of our middle brain called Thalamus that causes us to remember which is a wonderful blessing, there are, however, certain things in our past that our heart informs our brain to forget.

"...forgetting those things that are behind and reaching forward to those things that are ahead, I press toward the goal for the prize of the upward call of God in Christ Jesus,"

(Philippians 3:13-14).

Our spiritual eyes see through the eye of faith, our ears are tuned to the voice of the Spirit and our feet walk in step with God. But better still, the Lord opens the spiritual eyes of our heart. The wisest man who ever lived namely Solomon said these words-

"Keep your heart with all diligence, for out of it spring the issues of life. Put away from you a deceitful mouth, and put perverse lips far from you. Let your eyelids look right before you. Ponder the path of your

feet, and let all your ways be established. Do not turn to the right or the left; Remove your foot from evil,"

(Proverbs 4:23-27).

To *"Keep our heart with all diligence"* simply means to be industrious, hard working, assiduous, like we care for our garden not tolerating weeds, bugs or pests that hinder our spiritual growth, getting rid of anything that hinders us in being all we can be for Christ. It means to be earnest in application; this simply means to *"put on the whole armor of God"* but above all that, to know the God of the armor.

Paul mentions the helmet of salvation, anything less than this is being careless with our life and our soul, being untrue to self and deliberately choosing careless haphazard living. This is why we must make a covenant with our eyes to not look at anything that distracts or compromises our life with God or destroys our anointing by the indwelling presence of the Holy Spirit.

Pray Against the Spirit of Deceit

Diligence means to be unceasing or untiring, the spiritual admonition would be to be occupied or devoted to Jesus until He calls us out of this world. Solomon gives us a strong warning, to put away deceit. Deceit means we put forth a willing effort to deceive someone, to falsely misrepresent, habitual intentional fraud or betrayal, double-dealing. We are living in a day when we need to be spiritually focused on our relationship with God. The enemy goes *"to and fro throughout the earth seeking somebody to devour."*

How can we experience the peace of God when all around us we see the evidence of uncertainty, the results of evil, of injustices and unfairness, peoples rights being violated by some other person who holds control over them, or the forsaking of former principles or professions of faith vows, or the forsaking of covenant commitments of faith referred to as apostasy?

As Christians we must remain focused on Jesus Christ, to know what His Word is saying to us now! To maintain our priorities, to believe God for what He has promised and to realize that we are strangers and pilgrims in this world. To not allow anyone to mess up our life with God by robbing us of the greatest treasure any one person can experience as a free gift from God Himself, His peace and eternal salvation!

To better experience God's peace in a world of unrest and uncertainties, we must realize that we are not of this world and are merely passing through as a people on assignment for God's purpose to build His eternal Kingdom.

The *"peace of God within us,"* is beyond any human or intellectual understanding. Paul reminded us that it *"surpasses understanding,"* so how do we understand God's peace so that we might receive and experience this peace within our heart and mind, including every fiber of our being, our emotional make-up, especially during these troubled times when circumstances can rob us of so much so soon, keeping us from being a river overflowing with a testimony of God's peace in a world that knows no peace.

First of all, we must realize that this peace originates from God and is transferred from God by the Holy Spirit as a gift from God into our soul. For this peace to become real to us, we must believe and have faith in God for every detail of our spiritual well being both in this life and the life to come.

Our faith might be in place and our heart right with God, but what if our emotions react to unexpected situations which can result in turmoil as a result of all the uncertainties that affect us? This is God's purpose in providing His peace to stabilize our emotions as a result of our faith "in Christ," so that we might better experience His peace and live effective victorious lives before the world as a testimony of His life in us.

Our Position "in Christ" becomes our Spiritual Possession

We must have a heart-knowing faith that we are secure *"in Christ"* as a result of our position *"in Christ."* Our position *"in Christ"* always becomes our spiritual possession; we possess God's peace in our total being as our heavenly inheritance. The apostle Paul makes numerous reference to our position "in Christ" as our spiritual possession in his letter to the church at Ephesus.

> *"In Him you also trusted, after you heard the Word of truth, the gospel of your salvation; in whom also, having believed, you were sealed with the Holy Spirit of promise, who is the guarantee of our inheritance until the redemption of the purchased possession, to the praise of His glory,"*

(Ephesians 1:13-14).

Spiritual strength does not exist by our human effort, our nature or intellect, *"our strength comes from the Lord who made heaven and earth."* When God created us as individuals He already placed so much of Himself in us including His breath of life, but He wants to also provide us with eternal life. He can only do this with our permissive will. He will never force Himself upon us. He desires that we search for Him with all of our heart so that He might reveal Himself to us. He desires to become Lord of our life.

He had planned for His redeemed people to draw their spiritual strength, wisdom, power and direction from Him. We can only achieve this by knowing His Word and by living out of His Word by faith, our total dependence must be on the Lord for our total well being, we cannot take one step without Him or we lose our way.

Leaning on the everlasting arms simply means, by this, we are the most victorious, the happiest the most joyful, honest, the purist and undefiled people in the world, to have Jesus as the author and finisher of our life, as the "Prince of our Peace."

As a re-creation of God's grace we are now a living spirit with a body of flesh, *"created by Christ Jesus who walk not after the flesh,"* we have a *"living God"* to aid us and to sustain us to pursue the things of the Spirit. God knows us better than we know ourselves, who knows and understands our adversary. He knows the enemy is deceptive and that he desires to kill, steal, and destroy everything precious and beautiful, to rob us of having peace with God. God knows that the enemy of our soul is a cunning deceptive taskmaster. *"A father of lies"* that uses his victims to do his damnable work, an enemy to everything that is holy good and right. This present world has become the theater for his operations, our hope would be in vain had Jesus not interceded for us in defeating the enemy at the cross to destroy the works of the devil.

The struggles we encounter for the most part involves the problems we create for ourselves, by our disobedience, rather than to understand and receive by faith our position in the heavenly places in Christ. The entire concept of our position in Christ is all about a covenant relationship, this constitutes our freedom concerning the battles of the spirit, flesh and the mind, and we have an eternal inheritance that will not fade away reserved in heaven.

Were it not that the almighty God, the everlasting Father, the most powerful, *"above all principalities and powers"* were able *"to quench all the fiery darts of the wicked one"* protecting us with His shield of protection, we would be defeated and without hope in this world and doomed to eternal death with the wicked. As our shield of protection, the enemy's arrows fall to the ground as ineffective and we become more than conquerors through Christ.

Jesus said,

> *"He who believes in Me, as the Scriptures said, "From his innermost being shall flow rivers of living water." But this He spoke of the Spirit, whom these who believed in Him were to receive..."*

(John 7:38-39 NAS).

We all have the ability to become anything, and all we desire to be in Christ; He fashioned us this way, crafting us into His image by His Word, building potential into a product does not mean that potential will be fully revealed or accomplished. For example, a violin has to be crafted, but this involves process, it takes time, skill and patience including much hard work with perseverance, should I become discouraged and shelf the project, it will never become what it was designed to be, to make beautiful music, so it is with our lives, people become discouraged and they trash and shelf their potential because they do not understand either the magnitude of their ability or they fail to surrender to the Lordship of Christ, or they become discouraged and quit.

Antonio Stradivarius was a renowned violin maker having become known as one of the great violin builders of that period, never to be equaled, but had it not been for his predecessor and mentor Nicolo' Amati, Stradivarius would never have achieved his status for which he became known. Since that time there have been many copies of the Stradivarius models with many people being deceived in thinking they own such a valuable instrument when all they have is merely a copy of an original. As Christians, we are copies of the original, the only way to determine the original from the facsimile or fake is to see what is on the inside, just as with people, it may sound like an original and look authentic, even the label itself will not reveal the authenticity of the instrument, only when the violin is taken apart to probe the markings of the workmanship of the original builder can the true identity be discovered. I was about to discover this in the most unexpected way.

Unknown to me as I repaired the violin the old lady brought to my shop was the history and the value of what I held in my hands. The top had become unglued and the lady had informed me to take good care of it since it had belonged to her great grandfather who had won numerous awards. Why the builder carved the groves on the inside or back of the top made me curious, I even wondered why he had not smoothed it out as I did. I would discover my questions when the old lady came to pick it up and showed me the documentation including a photo; the violin had been crafted in the 1600's by a student of Antonia Stradivarius. I discovered that the groves greatly enhanced the tonal qualities of the violin and after I included them on my next violin the tonal quality increased better than fifty percent.

When I craft a violin the wood is in my command, surrendered to my will and purpose, it never argues with me or rebels, it simply submits and conforms to the work of my hands and is lifeless until placed into the hands of the master violinist who knows how to bring out the best performance and suddenly the atmosphere is filled with pleasing sounds that captures its audience with a standing ovation. When our natural state of being becomes conformed to the supernatural hands of the Master who positions us where we can produce beautiful music for His glory, then our lives will reach its ultimate potential and heaven stands in celebration.

Armor is meant for Soldiers

The apostle Paul wrote to the believers at Ephesus concerning the shield of faith and the armor of the Christian soldier. Paul wrote this letter while being chained to a Roman soldier and amidst the atmosphere of military sights and sounds which became very familiar to him, as did his chains that bound him in body while in his spirit; Paul was a free man in Christ as an ambassador in chains. Paul knew all about the armor of a soldier but his victory was in the God of the armor.

The Roman soldiers surrounding Paul had no idea that the power of God indwelt Paul as it did and that all this great gift of freedom, spiritual power, the forgiveness of sins and eternal peace was also available to them as well through the power of the cross of Jesus Christ.

As soldiers of the cross of Jesus Christ, we have an authorized delegated ministry to humanity, the highest and most honorable noble call than on any battlefield on this entire earth.

Only as we live by the Word of God will we experience the living Word working in our behalf, protecting, keeping and sustaining us with a peace of mind even though there is turmoil and battle sounds' bursting all around us.

When we live by the Word, we will experience the Word living in us and working for us. The Word uncovers sin, reveals the enemy's devices, the Word discovers the whole duty of man to God, the love of God for man, and through God's Word we discover our duty to God, to the gospel and to humanity. We discover God's grace, His strength and purpose for our lives and His promise to us as being faithful to His Word. By the Word of God the Holy Spirit goes to battle in our defense; the devil is defeated and our souls are comforted and secured and we stand in the righteousness of Christ before a holy God.

Through the years many vicious battles were fought but the greatest battle ever fought and won with complete victory standing apart as the mighty conqueror over sin and death completely defeating the enemy took place first in the mind and heart of God, and then in the Garden of Gethsemane, and finally on a hill called Golgotha where Jesus won the battle over all the devils and demons of hell to make us more than conquers through Him to secure our salvation.

In Philippians 4:6, Paul admonished the believer to be anxious for nothing. Our soul is never anxious; it is always our mind that allows us to become anxious or frustrated, which may in time affect our spirituality.

The joy of the Lord is always our spiritual strength that affects our physical make-up. In his letter to the Church at Philippi, Paul mentions joy and rejoicing fourteen times which always reflects the practical hope of the Christian.

Faith, trust and belief are all one and the same and flow out of our innermost being, our belief system; this becomes an expression of our heart and soul.

> "...*For out of the abundance of the heart the mouth speaks,*"

> (Matthew 12:34).

> "*Keep your heart with all diligence, for out of the heart are the issues of life,*"

> (Proverbs 4:23).

When all seems Lost

While riding around the Gulf area following hurricane Katrina, our team spotted a lady standing in her yard observing her loss. I felt led to approach her asking if she would desire our prayers. As we prayed over her she began to weep, she told us that the loss of her house was very minor that she had just gone through a divorce and her daughter had recently died.

She related to us how that she had not approved of her daughter's marriage which was not good and then one day in a fit of rage her daughter's husband doused her with lighter fluid setting her on fire, and as she lay on her hospital bed dying from sustaining severe burns, she asked me, "who are all these people dressed in white?" and then she passed away, now I have absolutely nothing left but Jesus in my heart.

With nothing but Jesus in our heart, we are still the riches people on earth. We never know what fate awaits us, we too may lose all our earthly possessions and all that is precious to us, but if we find ourselves standing on a lonely street homeless and friendless with Jesus in our heart, we are still the richest people on the earth!

If our only treasure in heaven is the treasure of our children and their children's children, then our heavenly inheritance is truly rich, people often say we will take nothing with us when we leave this earth, I choose to disagree! Do you realize that we can take our children with us to heaven and that we are responsible for the future generations that will be birthed out of our loins; this should prompt us to pray without ceasing for their spiritual well being.

Paul assures the believer that the power of God's presence and peace will guard not only the soul that lives in fellowship with Christ as safe and unharmed in spite of any conflict or assault from within or without and will bring even our rebellious minds into subjection to His will, to experience and have the mind of Christ, that is to say to think as Christ would think.

The Holy Spirit is in charge of our children and their children's children and our prayers for their spiritual well being will bear fruit because God hears and answers our faith prayer words in His name, as we pray generational blessings upon them because out of our being as parents will come forth a multiplied host of diverse individuals who one day will study their genealogy to discover they had fore-fathers that served the Lord and they want to pattern their lives according to their commitment of faith to Christ and the gospel. One of the greatest blessings of my life as a father was to be able to baptize every one of our children and to hear them confess Jesus Christ as their Savior, and to observe with great enthusiasm how they individually worked at processing their heritage of faith through their discovery years.

The New Heart Renews the Old Mind

To think as Christ would think is to know His Word and to know how to apply His Word to any given situation to experience a renewing of our mind, so that our new heart and renewed mind will not be in conflict or rebellion against the will of God.

This is why the Holy Spirit can enter the heart even when the door of the mind is closed because our heart hears His voice first before our mind can comprehend the message.

Conviction always begins in the heart; our soul always comprehends God through the eye of understanding or of heart-knowing which passes all the understanding of the natural mind. This becomes so vast and awesome that there are no words in the human vocabulary to explain what we feel in our spirit other than the tears that may flow out of our emotions. The new heart instructs the mind to always renew itself to be in obedience to God's will and Word.

"I will bless the Lord who has given me counsel; My heart also instructs me in the night seasons. I have set the Lord always before me; because He is at my right hand I shall not be moved. Therefore my heart

is glad, and my glory rejoices; My flesh also shall rest in hope. For you will not leave my soul in hell, nor will You allow Your holy One to see corruption. You will show me the path of life: In Your presence is fullness of joy: At Your right hand are pleasures forevermore,"

(Psalm 16:7-11).

We are sustained by Christ's resurrected power in us; this sets us apart and makes us different from the people of the world, the unbeliever. As Christians, we live by the power of Christ's resurrection. We are a people of faith that live in and by that power, it is His resurrected life power that sustains our faith and life which keeps us from falling or becoming dismayed. Even in death, we will still experience resurrection power, our body dies but our spirit lives on forever. We have no justifiable reason to ever become dismayed since God promised to take care of us and to see us through until the end, even through *"the valley of the shadow of death."*

Frugal people are always concerned with the integral details of their life because they value the gift of life. We have learned through experience that we must master the details of our life or they will master us, our thoughts are devoted to who we are and dominate our conversations and our decision making processes. This is an important aspect of who we are. This is why we have disciplined ourselves to always depend on the Lord for those things we cannot do for ourselves, and in that we depend upon His wisdom to have confidence in our circumstances. This is why we have learned to wait on the Lord; we learn that He renews our spiritual strength. That He is who He claims to be in every detail and we know that without Him we can do absolutely nothing. So we surrender to His Lordship as our Master.

Chapter Eight

Created by God's Design

Every person has a desire to discover their true identity, "You look just like your father and you even talk like him," these are familiar words that we have all heard; however, for the world to see Christ in us we must have the mind and Spirit of Jesus Christ within our heart for *"out of the heart are the issues of life."* We have been commissioned to speak for Him and to reflect His likeness.

When God said, *"Let us make man in Our own image, according to Our likeness;"* Jesus and the Holy Spirit were present and ever since the fall of man the Trinity has been working at restoring what was lost, to make it possible for the Christian to reveal their true identity.

The entire Life of Jesus Christ was set toward the cross to accomplish mans redemption, to die for the sins of the world and bring us back to God. He left His home in glory and the presence of everything holy, beautiful and heavenly to come to a sinful earth to take upon Himself the form of man, to become obedient unto death even the death of the cross, paying for a sin debt that He did not owe, but was willing to pay that debt so that we might be set free from sin and sins penalty to someday be exalted with Him in glory and share in the inheritance of heaven and all eternity. Jesus humbled Himself and became obedient to the death of the cross. By His death on the cross Jesus paid a debt He did not owe, He was buried in a grave that could not hold Him and came forth by His own power. To know what it means to have the mind of Christ, we too, have to surrender to God's will and be resurrected by His power, in life as in death.

Jesus Moved into Action

By His mighty power, Jesus would deliver individuals bound by satan's power, to liberate and set captives free from sin and shame. He came to seek and to save that which was lost, to save people from their sins, to deliver them from disease and death, to conquer the forces of evil, to defeat the devil and his cohorts, the most powerful mighty conquering saving power that heaven could provide came to our human rescue, nothing else was needed, and heaven and earth have not been the same since His appearing.

Jesus is the first Word and the Last Word to everything. His conquering power is working within our spirit and we will not give in or give up. Rather than thinking about taking our life into our own hands, we will surrender our life to Him. He is still doing His best work today by taking care of you and me and all His redeemed ones. If the world's financial empires fall, they had no spiritual foundation to begin with, and anything apart from spiritual is evil and corrupt. This world system never gives Jesus Christ honorable mention or respect, this present evil world is doomed to destruction as a kingdom of darkness.

"The wicked will be turned into hell, and all the nations that forget God,"

(Psalms 9:17).

Jesus is the answer for today's world. He always was and always will be. The Prince of Light has overthrown the prince of darkness making an eternal statement of His supremacy over the enemy of the souls of men. Jesus is the power of God at work in the world today! This goes beyond the intelligence of human knowledge or understanding, no human force has the ability to hold back the power of God or the Holy Spirit from breaking into the depth of a soul to redeem that life from destruction. Saving a soul from eternal damnation and holding on to that soul with a firm grip so strong that He said, *"No man will pluck them out of My Fathers hand."*

This reality should motivate us to look beyond this life including our present interests; our wimpy shallow faith, and our carnal accomplishments, including our earthly attachments or situations, and be willing to make whatever sacrifice necessary for the Holy Spirit to accomplish God's will in our lives, even if that means denying ourselves anything earthly, to detach ourselves from any or all earthly treasures of this world with a willingness to surrender to Christ's Lordship even if that means paying the ultimate sacrifice for His purpose and glory.

We can never submit to the Lordship of Christ until we see Him in all of life through the eyes of faith and to know Him in our heart, to possess Him in our soul and spirit with a clean heart and a renewed mind. When this is in place, we are carried up to that infinite height where Christ had been from eternity past in the bosom of the Father, and where He will reveal to us the glory He had with the Father from the beginning to share that glory with us the redeemed; an eternal inheritance that will never fade away and is there reserved and waiting for us upon our arrival.

So then, how does one deal with the uncertainty of the times in which we live, the fear of losing retirement benefits and investments. Does it bring a sense of fear into your spirit, and how do you work at overcoming all the uncertainties facing you today?

"For God has not given us the spirit of fear, but of power and of love and of a sound mind"

(2 Timothy 1:7).

"There is no fear in love; but perfect love casts out fear, because fear has torment. But he who fears is not made perfect in love,"

(1 John 4:18).

The spirit that God has placed within the believer is not one of "cowardice," or of shirking from duty, it is a spirit of power from on high. It is a spirit of power that will defy and defeat any or all opposing forces.

- ➢ power to speak powerful, effective, positive words of life into our situation,
- ➢ power to keep silent and wait on the Lord when every fiber in our being desires to speak out, give up or rebel,
- ➢ power of endurance at any or all cost even when we feel like giving up in defeated surrender,
- ➢ power of hope and restoration, that comes from beyond ourselves,
- ➢ power to do battle, by surrendering our battle to the Lord,
- ➢ power to love, beyond any human love as Christ loves us,
- ➢ power for a sound mind, like that of Christ Himself,
- ➢ power that seeks not its own will and way, but power to surrender without reservation.

This is a "determined love power" given by God and maintained by the Holy Spirit, so strong it never seeks its own but results in casting out any foreign intruder, any vain imagination or thoughts, maintaining a tranquil peace that passes any or all human understanding, with a spiritual healthy, sound and well balanced mind that is now in communication with the new heart that is in tune with the Holy Spirit of God, which thinks not in the realm of the flesh, but of the Spirit with a vigorous commitment dedicated to our call of duty for God's glory. The only way we can realize and appreciate the full impact of our spiritual maintenance is to daily become absorbed in God's Holy Word, to learn to pray with breakthrough power with a spirit of full surrender to His Lordship, knowing in our heart that our life is all about His life in us.

So what is our call to duty, but to have the mind of Christ and to do the will of God? We have this treasure in earthen vessels, a treasure of God's trust in us, the soul that strongly believes and loves may hope with confidence to someday see what we believe through the eye of faith, to be able to love as God loves and to rejoice with Him with unspeakable joy.

Whatever conflicts, hazards, pitfalls, hindrances or obstacles and concerns, whether inward or outward, whatever temptations or endurance, including insecurities concerning the salvation of our soul, our well being while we live on this earth, including our departure, does not depend upon our wisdom or strength, but upon our total surrender to what He desires to do in us, and what He will work out in us, and through us, and that for Himself and His eternal purpose for bringing us into the world.

As created by God, we are God's design and workmanship. We are God's redeemed property even in spite of our unfaithfulness, our insecurities and our childish ways.

Amidst the haunting shadows of life, including all the things that have hindered us and stood in our pathway, we can still say we know in whom we have believed and trusted our life, our soul, our whole being, and we are fully persuaded that God is able to keep us and our confession of faith in Him until that day when He calls our name and raptures us from this world into His glorious presence for all eternity in a world that never ends.

> *"You will show me the path of life; in Your presence is fullness of joy; at Your right hand are pleasures forever more,"*

(Psalm16:11).

From the very first moment we were born into this world, the Holy Spirit of God hovers over us and anxiously awaits the moment He can enter our heart by our invitation so that we might operate out of His anointed power.

In our counseling ministry, we have experienced that if we take individuals to the root of their problem and we introduce Jesus into the problem, the problem is soon redeemed, and relationships are restored.

The young couple had been married for three years and their love for each other had obviously deteriorated, and after listening to each of them vent their grievances, Anna Mary and I anointed both of them praying over them and when I said, "You don't have a marital problem, but you are resisting a call of God on your lives," the young man responded by saying, "How did you know that?" We challenged them to take advantage of the first counseling opportunity that presented itself and pursue a counseling ministry. Every evening for three weeks we received their call telling us of their new found love for each other and for the Lord. We were not surprised when they informed us that their best friends were planning to separate and the husband had already begun the divorce proceedings. "What shall we do?" was their question. Our counsel was to encourage them to pray with their friends and to hold off on the divorce.

By this time the wife who was being divorced had moved to another state to live with her parents, but in a matter of just one week she was sitting in our living room seeking counsel, the next week her husband joined her in our home. My first comment was, "Man you have a problem." He looked at me as if to say, "of course I do, that's why I'm here." I informed him by saying, your problem is a generational matter, you have an anger problem," I asked, "did your father have this problem?" He informed me that not only did his father but also his grand-father. We prayed that the Holy Spirit would break the generational curse and encouraged the young couple to allow time to be their healer. Weeks went by and we received another call from the lady who informed us that her husband had decided to leave her and she needed counsel and prayer. Our intercessory prayer group was meeting at the church that evening and we invited her to join us. When she walked into the room, I informed those present about the problem and suggested that we pray in agreement that when the lady returns to her friend's house following our pray time that her husband would call to inform her that he decided to cancel the divorce and wants to make the marriage work. We had been home for about a half hour when the phone rang, the voice said, "David you won't believe what just happened, my husband called and said he tore up the papers and wants me to come home, we are going to make our marriage work." That's more than three years ago and the young couple is still together.

Jesus said, *"If we lay hands on the sick they will recover."* There is absolutely nothing more emotionality hurtful and spiritually harmful than a broken relationship, be that in Christ or in marriage, in both situations, certainly not all is well or it wouldn't hurt and harm so many individuals. Jesus came, *"to bring peace on earth good will toward men."* Giving Jesus ownership of our problems is the least we can do no matter what that problem might be so that He might reveal His supernatural power in us and among us.

Having a Surrendered Heart

Thousands of people die every day and miss their moment of salvation. Either they have never heard the gospel story or they simply didn't care, or they failed to understand the simple message of salvation.

From the beginning of creation following Adams transgression, God promised a redeemer to show us not only the way of life but to become our very life and bring peace to this earth.

God sent His One and only Son into the world to save our soul from eternal destruction. Jesus Christ is our only way to God and heaven and the only way we can have peace with God, with ourselves and everything around us.

It takes less than thirty seconds to say, "Jesus come into my heart and save my soul, I am sorry for my sins, I believe you are the Son of God, I confess that I am a sinner and I want to be born again." This confession of faith in Jesus Christ will change our eternal destiny, from spiritual death to eternal life with God.

We should never discourage even a small child from wanting to ask Jesus to come into their heart; we should do everything we can to help shape and mold their spiritual life in Jesus Christ. The older a person becomes the more difficult it is to win them to Christ.

Even though a parent may experience the peace of God and live a devoted life as a Christian for many years, we are elevated to a new level of praise, peace and joy when we see our loved ones surrendering their heart and life to the Lord and to know that the same convictions that He birthed in us He will bring forth in them.

If you are struggling with unsaved loved ones allow me to encourage you to never give up! As long as there is life there is hope. In our ministry, we have wept with mothers, who were burdened for the spiritual well being of their lost children or grandchildren. Some of those mothers were called home to heaven and never saw their children saved, but we did, we saw them surrender their lives to Jesus Christ. Some of those children are now adults and in full time ministry today, it would have been even more joyful if those mothers could have witnessed the salvation of their children, but one day they will be reunited forever in heaven.

The greatest blessings we can place upon a child are our anointed prayer words in the name of Jesus. The Holy Spirit will take our prayers to flight, God will discharge His answer from His Throne in heaven and they will experience peace in their heart, and will know that someone prayed.

The only way to experience peace with God is to completely surrender our whole being to the Lordship of Jesus Christ. If we are troubled in our spirit about anything, this may well affect our emotions, our emotions may affect our health, and our health may affect our faith and jeopardize our commitment to Christ and the enemy will take us on a downward spiral before we know what happened.

Be true to yourself. Take inventory of your spiritual life, bow your head in prayer and call on the name of Jesus. He is waiting to hear from you, He will hear and answer our prayer. He will forgive our sins, this is why He came to this earth, trust Him! It is what He does best!

His Spirit is Our Strength

"But you shall receive power when the Holy Spirit has come upon you; and you shall be witnesses to Me in Jerusalem, and all Judea and Samaria and to the end of the earth,"

(Acts1:8).

No matter what our situation might be, it is good to know that we are not alone, God is with us, His Holy Spirit dwells in us, our friends are for us and we draw strength from each another. As God's people, we have a liberating spiritual force inside of us that empowers our mind and spirit to be more than conquers, that power involves our total surrender to the mighty power of God as He conquers in our behalf.

God always maintains what He has created through His Word, and we, as His creation are being kept by the Power and promise of that Word. His Spirit within our spirit becomes a liberating force preventing us from becoming captives to our circumstances. God wants to empower us to be revealed from within us, we are the people He has chosen to carry His presence in our world today as an extension of His love. We are responsible not only for our generation, but that future generations might also know the Lord.

"Who are kept by the power of God through faith for salvation ready to be revealed in the last time,"

(1 Peter 1:5).

God's mercies are renewed every morning, and He wants to do a renewed work in us and our age is no factor. He is not through with us yet! He knows we have much to offer to our generation, because we have years of experience in living for Him. The aging process has mellowed us providing us with wisdom and understanding and His creativity in us never ceases. His life in us does not allow us to stalemate or to become stagnate. Everyday He wants to take us to a new level of relationship with Himself leading us to those persons we are meant to influence by His Spirit. We are still clay in the hands of the potter and for many of us who have endured hardship and disappointments; these are the best years of our life to make our statement of faith for God's glory.

Time has not only aged many of us it has made us tuff and strong to endure hardship with a proven faith that has worked every time because He always brought us through. When our focus is on what Jesus desires to do in us and through us, we lose sight of our feeble ways and learn to live and move by His supernatural power from within us as an overflowing vessel for His glory.

We are as Light Shining in a Dark Place

According to science, nothing travels faster than light; illumination is the opposite of darkness. An artist always accents light to draw the attention of the beholder to the focal point so as to highlight the main subject. Light in scripture always refers to Jesus Christ who came as Light to the world but before He left this earth, He told His followers that now they are lights to the world. Light in scripture is always associated with truth, and God as Light will continue to shine forever; since we are light the Holy Spirit collectively places us in position to cause His light to shine through us, to conquer the world with the widest expanse as searchlights being a symbol of God's presence as we represent Him to our world.

> *"Behold You desire truth in the inward parts and in the hidden part You will make me to know wisdom. Purge me with hyssop, and I shall be clean, wash me, and I shall be whiter than snow,"*

(Psalm 51:6-7).

There is life in light; this is why we place the flowers on the window sill toward the sunlight since plants will always lean toward the light. If you ever had the opportunity to dive into the depth of the sea you will also discover that plant-life thrives as a result of light penetrating through the darkness.

There is no night of the soul so dark that the Light of God's love cannot penetrate through to bring about a spirit of renewal and encouragement. When we allow Jesus Christ to take complete control of everything we are about, everything will work for our good. God made Jesus everything that He is about, from eternity to eternity. We see the name of Jesus interwoven in all of God's activities; we see His majestic beauty in the absolute perfection of God. Jesus was completely surrendered to His Father's will, to honor and identify with the Father in all the activity of the Godhead, as He walked among men and ministered for His Father's glory, in life as in death, He sought not his own will, but that of His father in heaven. His resurrection power witnessed to the mighty power of God as the origin and only source of life.

"In Him was life, and the life was the light of men. And the light shines in the darkness, and the darkness did not comprehend it,"

(John 1:4-5).

To obtain eternal life from God, we are invited to give up our life for His life, to die is to gain and to lose is to win, to accept is to receive and to consecrate our life to Him is to discover His life of holiness. To surrender our life for His is to become the most powerful task force on the earth, as we serve Him with a united effort as a people from all nationalities, kindred, tongue and nations, becoming a collective body, a glorious church committed to live by His Word, to carry the banner of His name and in His name and through His power, reconcile the world unto Him as His faithful witness on the earth, joining hands with the millions who have served before us in centuries past, who also learned the power of calling upon His name in their time of need making good His Word, *"I will never leave you nor forsake you,"* and to do, *"exceedingly abundantly above all we can ask or think."* With open everlasting arms receiving all who will come to Him by faith anytime, anywhere, in any situation just as we are to instill in us a faith unshakeable and unmovable, a rock-solid sure foundation living our lives as a testimony for future generations to follow in our footsteps and spread the message of hope in God through Christ.

If there is evidence of generational curses, we will break them in Jesus' name and speak generational blessings upon our children and their children's children into future generations, realizing that should the world stand, nations will be birthed from out of our loins to also receive the truth, that Jesus came to remove the curse for sin for all mankind in every generation of time to be set free indeed!

Chapter Nine

Our Heritage of Faith

Our heritage of faith always provides us with people who serve as role models or as spiritual significant others. We all have someone that showed us the way to Christ, someone we looked up to that we admired for the way they exemplified their faith and how they lived before God and man; how that inspired and influenced us to live in such a way that others will come to know Christ and to also leave a legacy of faith after we leave this world.

The people that have influenced our faith may be unknown to the world but there was something special about who they were and still are; it may not have been their words that influenced us, but just the way they lived their lives and we found ourselves saying, "I want to be like that person."

We should always keep a record of these people and never fail to thank them for their spiritual influence. They might be greatly encouraged if they would know how influential they have been and how we were encouraged by their testimony, how their invested interests in the gospel helped to motivate and shape our spirituality and commitment to the cause of Christ.

These people become spiritual significant others in our life; they encourage and motivate us; they cause us to establish high goals for who we want to become in life. This is what the world is looking for, roll models that will make Jesus Christ real to them.

I remember as a small boy when tourists would stop by the farm to enjoy the Amish way of life. One day Red Skelton, a Hollywood comedian, visited the farm and while in conversation with my father, Mr. Skelton said, "you folks have what the world is looking for, a peaceful tranquil lifestyle," I saw tears trickling down his face, my father stood straight and erect with his arms folded across his chest and a smile on his face, he didn't have to say anything in response because the smile on his face reflected his heritage of faith and I saw something of great value that day in the silent language of the soul. My Dad was drawing from a deep well of family heritage of faith and no words were needed to respond to a positive comment.

Those were the days when life seemed innocent and tranquil, to spend a day by the meadow stream fishing, and watching the water as it cascaded over the water wheel, dreaming about what we want to do with our lives, not even being aware that all the while our lives were being shaped by a lifestyle that is unique. A silent persuasive example of living separate from the world with a dedication for what is right. Now that we are all getting older, that simple child-like faith and trust is still the heartbeat of our soul, to live separate from the world with the longings for a better world, courage to face our challenges and our aspirations for undisturbed peace, for our promised eternity with God.

We all draw strength from our heritage of faith. We have mental pictures as we remember mother as she sat in her rocking chair reading her Bible. As a boy, I decided I wanted to marry someone like my mother, not only for the reason that she was a wonderful provider, but I saw so much of God in her. That dream and desire became fulfilled by God bringing a godly woman into my life to become my partner in faith, in life and in ministry. I observed mother as she desired a greater faith to reach into her unknown future for more of God's peace, to sustain her for the day, as she prayed for the fruit of her womb with thoughts and prayers, concerning her future generations, that they, too, might experience the blessings of God to live their lives for Him.

The day would come when I saw that faith and peace played out as a silent testimony and witness that allowed her to endure hardship, sickness and disappointments as well as the joys and aspirations of life. To be committed to her marriage, to see all her children come to know the Lord and to still intercede in prayer daily by name for everyone of her many off-springs, to still be active by taking care of herself now in her ninety eighth year.

She honored her parents by living a holy life with the promise from God's Word for a long and prosperous life; Married at the young age of eighteen and giving birth to four children she never traveled far and most of her life was lived on the same farm yet she touched the world with her influence, she has become an old saint of God, a spiritual icon to her friends and family. Little did she realize that out of her loins would come forth business men, professional artisans, teachers and preachers, ranch owners, world travelers, missionaries that touched the world, including company and corporate executives, an army of dedicated soul-winners that would impact the Kingdom of God on the earth, and since its an on-going story, the rest of the story only eternity will reveal!

Our service for Christ on this earth does not reach its completion on this earth. It's just the beginning of something eternal that we can only grasp by faith. A continuation of an activity destined for eternity that had its origin in a parent's heart as they prayed for their children to be kept by the power of almighty God."

When the world sees that we are truly different and set apart, even though they may not know or understand the well of "Water of Life" from which we draw and drink, or who our life source is, the world and unbelievers will see our light source shining in a dark place and they will be influenced even though we may never say a word.

The Holy Spirit will always place us in a position to be light to the world, a position of great responsibility. If there were no darkness in the world, there would be no need for light. Our light to the world will always shine brightest when we don't say anything, but in a humble way live out our testimony without compromise and become as a Bible that other people might read.

Becoming First Responders for Jesus

My first experience in seeing someone die happened the day we moved to Tennessee to begin our pastoral ministry. The north-bound car came across the medium and into our path stopping short of hitting our vehicle; bodies were thrown everywhere, I saw limbs detached from the bodies and the first person I assisted was a small boy, as he looked into my eyes while I held him in my arms I told him that Jesus loves him and will take care of him. He died while I held him; this would be an experience I will never forget. Five people died that day all because someone had a drinking problem. My compassion for a dying world increased that day with a renewed desire to become an extension of who Jesus desires to be through us, even to complete strangers.

Jesus always wants to enlarge Himself in us so that He might increase Himself on the earth through us; this is why He positions us with an assignment in specific geographical locations to become an extension of who He is, where we work and the people we meet on a daily basis, are all a part of His design for us. He supplies us with all the resources we need to complete our assignment with both physical and spiritual strength, and the Holy Spirit enlarges our territory. A good example of this is as young people pursue their educational careers by moving to different parts of the world to meet their life's companion complimenting their future generations by enlarging their realm of influence.

Our oldest son Melvin did an in-depth research study on our ancestry; he discovered many good characters evolved out of that, he also discovered some shady characters that helped us to understand why we encountered personal struggles and the dynamics behind our personal characteristics.

My grandfather Huyard was not an original Amishman. He was a school teacher in the public school system who met the Amish bishop's daughter, Mary. They fell in love and were married, that meant grandfather who was a Lutheran by faith became an Amishman. In time, he purchased a huge tract of land and divided the land for several of his sons which are still in the possession of his third and forth generations.

To better understand who I am and what I felt God wants to be in me, I traced my granddads heritage which took me to the Swiss-German border of the Huguenot community, in that, I discovered that my violin making and art ability came out of that heritage. It also helped me to better understand some of my personal spiritual struggles that warred against me.

What we shall become in Christ transcends all our expectations and overwhelms our capacity to even comprehend the eternity of activity God has planned for us. If we bring with us traces of generational traits or curses or undesirable habits, Jesus breaks the curse for sin when we receive Him into our heart and we become new creations in Christ. And the things we desired to love to do that stemmed from generations past will be broken by the power of the blood and the life that we now live; we live by faith in the Son of God who loves us so very much and we become an instrument for His glory.

When we come into the Lord's presence in praise and worship heaven stands at attention. The angels and the heavenly hosts are engaged in celebration. Their harps are always tuned and ready to rejoice. There is more rejoicing in heaven over one sinner that repents than ninety nine righteous people who need no repentance.

Statistics reveal that every twenty four hours 250,000 people die world-wide. Referring to His Kingdom Jesus said, *"Few there be that find it."*

If ten percent of these people are saved think of the multitude of people that enter heaven in each twenty four hour period of earthly time. Along with all those that are being saved, along with all the prayers that are ascending and everything else that happens in heaven, even though we can only imagine what is taking place in the spirit realm it causes us to rejoice with a determined faith to accomplish our assignment on the earth for Christ.

Since God's peace reigns within our spirit, the forces of evil that oppress us have to take their leave, the power and presence of the Holy Spirit is over us and all around us, it is too much for the enemy and he moves into his place and the keeping power of God conquers over the enemy.

God's peace is beyond explanation, but so very real. Just to mention and plead the power of the blood of Jesus over our situation causes every demon to take their flight and invokes heaven to stand at attention. We are drawn into a realm of hallelujah bliss as the Lord sends forth our prayer requests to accomplish our desires and God's peace comes to earth. His Kingdom comes to earth as it is in heaven, breaking our bondage; to bring complete freedom and deliverance into any situation; nothing is too hard for God to set captives free from the vices of sin and spiritual death.

We Are a Persuaded People

We are a persuaded peace loving people knowing that *"Greater is He that is in us than he that is in the world."* We are persuaded that Jesus Christ is able to keep us from indifference, apostasy, backsliding or rebellion, from sin!

The reason that I am so excited about life in Jesus Christ is for the fact I have become persuaded in my heart and mind, that Jesus is my best Friend. He has delivered us from many dangerous situations. He has always been there when we needed Him. He made good on His Word, and He makes life so very exciting. His imparted peace and joy, His felt expressed love and care is beyond explaining or description! When we don't know how to pray, all we have to do is speak His name, we have avoided what might have been disastrous situations and all we could say was, "Jesus!", and we always know that we were delivered by His outstretched arm. This is all the more reason for us to guard that which we have committed unto Him until that day when He takes us out of this present evil world and ushers us into His eternal Kingdom.

Peace loving people have a Spirit overflow, an anointing of the Holy Spirit. It is the gift and fruit of the Holy Spirit controlling our lives, every fiber of our being, even our countenance glows with His presence.

"Therefore let that abide in you which you heard from the beginning. If what you heard from the beginning abides in you, you will abide in the Son and in the Father. And this is the promise that He has promised us-eternal life. These things I have written to you concerning those who try to deceive you. But the anointing which you have received from Him abides in you, and you do not need that anyone teach you; but as the same anointing teaches you concerning all

*things, and is true, and is not a lie, and just as it has
taught you, you will abide in Him,"*

(1 John 2:24-27).

We Are Anointed by God

The anointing allows us to do for God and for ourselves
including others what we could never do on a human level
by our own strength. The anointing empowers us by the Holy
Spirit operating through us; the anointing seals our identity
and fully persuades us that we belong to God.

Jesus said, *"Because I live, you shall live also,"*
(John 14:19).

Living in the power of Christ's resurrection is living on
the very threshold of eternity. The day of our demise when
we leave this earth is not about saying goodbye, it is all about
saying hello, it is not about weeping, but about shouting, not
about lamenting, but to rejoice.

The difficulties we face in life should only draw us closer
to Jesus Christ who is our deliverer. Christ's own resurrection
causes us to triumph over death, Christ's victory over death
and the grave becomes our victory because of His Spirit Life
in us, this makes spiritual death void and cancelled with a
transition to life eternal where we shall live eternally and
never die.

Heart-Knowing Peace

Life's experiences, that we have encountered, have
taught us to conquer through our faith in God, as a result of
where we have been and all that He has brought us through.
We have all walked a path in our life that was not pleasant,

yet in that experience we have learned to know Him as in no other way. There is just no way to explain what transpires as we find ourselves on a hospital bed and are at the mercy of God's grace and the people who minister to us, along with the people we love, somebody is doing for us what we cannot do for ourselves and we know we are not only at the mercy of those caregivers around us, our faith in Jesus Christ and His healing power sustains us and we hear His voice speaking into our spirit as in no other way. This is the reason that we do not allow ourselves to become overwhelmed with fear because God says, *"Fear not, perfect love casts out fear."*

Everything about God and our relationship with Him is supernatural. He provides us with supernatural ability, protection and peace. Every time a national tragedy occurs, people tend to panic, becoming fearful. September 11, 2001, was a good example. Many of us lost large amounts of our investments that were meant to see us through our sunset years, but by God's grace and His rich supply, we are all still making it. Our faith has been in God to provide for us and He will always see us through. He hears and answers our prayers for His help and wisdom.

The world does not understand this because the world is identified with the kingdom of darkness, the natural reaction for the people of the world is to panic when tragedy happens and will even curse God.

Anna Mary and I experienced this first hand as we sat on board a United flight at Dulles International Airport that was scheduled to depart for Denver at 9:00 am. Our first awareness of a problem came about as people answered their cell phones informing them that a Plane had flown into the World Trade Center in New York. All we knew was that a tragedy had taken place not realizing the extent of the disaster.

We were soon informed to deplane and evacuate the terminal, without any forethought, we reacted out of our spiritual instinct and the leading of the Holy Spirit in our life. People around us were in a state of panic, everyone was running and the noise level was very high, we heard only a few people praying asking the Lord to help them.

Together we raised our hands in prayer, praying out loud as we walked around the terminal building in the main Gate area. We were the last to shuttle to the main terminal building and there again we continued to pray for the people keeping sight of each other so as not to loose each other.

We both sensed an overwhelming peace coming over us and the best way to describe what we felt was as if someone had placed a warm blanket over us. "Do you feel as if you are walking in a bubble?" I asked Anna Mary; she too, felt what I felt as we walked all over the lower level of the main terminal building.

Not until everyone had been evacuated did we step outside only to discover that all Shuttle busses and most of the taxi drivers had also left. "Now what are we going to do?" We did what comes natural for a Christian; we again raised our hands toward heaven in an audible voice and prayed, "Lord send someone to help us!"

Before I could say amen, a gentleman stepped in front of me asking. "What do you think about what is taking place, where are you from and where were you going?" I answered the questions and remarked, "If we could only get a Taxi to take us to a car Rental Agency." Another gentleman dressed in black stepped forward seemingly out of nowhere and remarked, "I'm Charles King, I own the Dulles taxi system, please step into my car." I had not noticed the TV camera person that was broadcasting the event. Mr. King assisted us as we checked with every Rental Agency in that entire area to no avail, "Well, I'll just have to take you back to the Valley myself," Mr. King remarked.

We arrived at our house around 4:00 pm and not until we turned on the TV did we realize the extent of what all had taken place that day. It was only then that we were able to contact our daughter Crystal who lives in Steamboat and had been waiting for us in Denver since we had planned to spend some time with her and Kendra, Crystal's daughter.

Our Son Dale also lives in Colorado and knew Crystal and Kendra had spent the night in a motel in the Denver area, knowing now that all flights were grounded. He stopped by the Motel to inform Crystal that we would not be arriving. "Turn on the TV," Dale said. It was only now that our children realized what had taken place that morning.

While they were watching the events unfold the news reporter announced that the United Flight from Dulles that had departed at 9:00 am had just crashed in western Pennsylvania. "Dad and Mom were on that flight!" Crystal remarked, thinking we too had perished until they saw their Dad being interviewed at Dulles International by a news reporter.

In appreciation for our ride back to the valley, I told the taxi driver to present Mr. King with one of my paintings. Mr. King expressed his gratitude in a letter several weeks later and said, the hour he spent with us that day as he tried to help us were the most peaceful moments he had ever experienced, yet we had said very little.

We all have been in situations that caused our faith and trust in the Lord to mature. So why include a personal story of challenge? Simply for the sake of encouragement, we all have our faith stories that taught us trust, patience and hope in God.

"Are you fearful about the unknown, about your future well being, your financial situation, even your spirituality?" God allows by His permissive will for situations to come into our lives to lift us to a higher level of experience and dependence, of faith and trust in Him. Think of your experiences as God preparing you for something special and important and receive into your spirit the following words from God's Word for you today, right now!

"…Who have been upheld by Me from birth, who have been carried from the womb: Even to your old age, I am He and even to gray hairs I will carry you! I have made, and I will bear; even I will carry, and deliver you,"

(Isaiah 46:3-4).

To know God personally is the greatest blessing anyone person could ever hope for, God who by His Word created all things, who wrote our name in the palm of His hand before He created the world, who sustains us by His grace. The God of the universe who always was and who always will be loves us. His greatest mission to earth was to bring peace to this earth and save our lost soul, to receive us into His eternal presence and glory.

Just the idea that we can actually converse with Him, that He actually hears our voice that He knows us by name, and watches over us with His tender loving care seems to good to be true, but its true!

To feel the sanctifying process of His holiness; working His grace in our behalf through the Holy Spirit in us, as we live out our life of faith in Him. He is preparing us for an eternity with Him.

God is still revealing His power, purpose and glory, inviting all people to come to learn to know Him in a personal way and He makes Himself known through the following ways.

> ➢ through the natural world,
> ➢ through His Son Jesus Christ as the Word made flesh,
> ➢ through the inspired Word, the Bible,
> ➢ through the fathers by the prophets,
> ➢ through the witness of the believers,

> ➤ through His attributes,
> ➤ through the Holy Spirit,
> ➤ through His body, the church.

We should never underestimate the power of God and how He chooses to make Himself known. He breaks through every barrier of doubt and unbelief, as long as there is life in a person, there is hope in God. When God brings conviction to an individual, the forces of hell cannot stand against that person and God's Holy Spirit and His amazing grace.

To know God is to know God's will for our life. To know God by faith in Christ, and to act out of that faith, to know God is to experience His power and favor, to know God is knowing Him by our heart-knowing intellect.

We can know God by His power in us, as He strengthens us by that power even in our weakest moments. We can know we are strong in Him and He provides us with His overcoming power and ability.

We can know God only through God's Son Jesus Christ, and when we know Him our spiritual life permeates with a life-light force and a passion that comes from our inner self, and beyond ourselves with a faith anchored and motivated by the power we receive by believing Him for what He says in His Word.

To know God is to be rooted in Him, grounded in the love He gives to overflowing with a witness that He is real, that He can be felt and known.

It is not complicated to know God; in fact it is so simple millions miss it. This is why our message of the gospel must be clear, plain, redemptive and simple. Theologians many times complicate the message; but communicators make it very simple, so simple a child can know God in a very real way.

Many individuals have discovered God when they were all alone; millions more have discovered Him at an old fashioned altar. The discovery of God is an individual matter and a personal decision. The Holy Spirit is God's agent in the world to convict of sin and bring the individual to a saving knowledge of Himself.

The greatest void anyone can experience is when God is seemingly absent, when there is no felt presence of the Holy Spirit. The gospel is God's power unto salvation, the gospel is the message of the cross, where sinners are invited to bring their worst, just as they are, to receive God's best that God has provided through His Son Jesus Christ to become filled with the power of the Holy Spirit.

Without the Holy Spirit we are Empty

On one of my missionary trips to Trinidad, we were invited to attend a Hindu service. I had never experienced such an absence of the Holy Spirit in my entire life. I watched in despair as individuals worshiped their false gods. The people were very kind and generous; in fact they were so generous that several came to hear the gospel where I was preaching, and as a result of this, several young people came forward and gave their lives to Jesus Christ.

Several years following my crusade to Trinidad, a teenage girl whose name was Charmin called me; she had moved to New York City and wanted to let me know that she was still serving the Lord, that is more than thirty years ago, but I still remember her name.

My involvement in ministry to Trinidad came about as Pastor Thomas Balchan listened to our radio broadcasts. On several occasions He invited me to come and minister to the four congregations that he had started having been converted from Hinduism to Christianity. South Trinidad consisted of a large population of people of East Indian decent.

A Baptist Pastor from our area expressed an interest in also broadcasting the gospel on the West Indies station from where our broadcasts were being transmitted, we assisted him in having his own program and he was now also receiving invitations to come to Trinidad which he accepted, following his first visit to Trinidad he invited Pastor Thomas to come to our area. For several months we arranged meetings in both Tennessee and Pennsylvania for Pastor Thomas to speak and to raise money for a worship Center in Trinidad since all four congregations had no buildings for their worship services and were meeting under the Palm tress.

Now my Baptist friend and I are invited to come for the dedication service for the new worship center, I mentioned our plans at a service where I was preaching and invited the congregation to donate clothing along with soap and tooth-paste not realizing that they would provide me with ten suit-cases full of items.

When we arrived at the primitive airport in Trinidad Pastor Thomas and members of his congregation were there to greet us, when they saw all of our luggage Pastor Thomas informed us that we would have to pay duty on all the items, we were not prepared to do that and he also informed us that they didn't have enough of money to pay for the tax on the items which could involve several hundred dollars.

I was also informed that we would need work permits to enter the country which we did not have. The officials placed our luggage on a primitive board platform and began to open the suitcases of the people in front of us, we had no idea what was about to happen, but we were all praying. "Do you have any tobacco or alcohol in your suitcases?" the officer asked. I told him that we didn't and than he said, "Move this stuff out of here." He never opened one suitcase.

As I approached the immigration officer he asked in a stern voice, "What are you doing sir?" I replied, "I'm sketching your portrait." I had taken my sketch pad to make notes for future paintings and decided this would be a good place to begin. Now the officer is all excited and calls for everyone's attention saying, "We have an artist here and he is sketching my face, come on in sir! Welcome to Trinidad, be our guest." I presented him with my crude sketch and we were soon on our way.

I had heard missionaries say that the Lord can make blind eyes see and also make seeing eyes blind.

Chapter Ten

Extensions of Jesus

J esus Christ came into this world to reveal the love that the father has for a lost and dying world. He came to seek and to save that which was lost and bring us to God providing us with everlasting life. He left this world and sent the Holy Spirit to lead, guide and direct us through life on earth, to empower us with delegated authority to represent Him on this earth and usher us into His eternal presence.

One of the greatest oppositions Jesus faced while in this world was the religious system which was committed to keeping the law; and rejecting His new dispensation of grace which is greater than our sin. Paul said,

"For the law of the Spirit of life in Christ Jesus has made me free from the law of sin and death,"

(Romans 8:2).

Christianity is more than a religion; it is a personal relationship that leads to a fulfilling, overflowing eternal life in Christ. Religion by itself may attempt to make Jesus for what He is not; refusing to accept Him for who He is, including His life changing power.

Religion may recognize God as the creator and the ruler of the universe, being an organized system of doctrine with an approved pattern of behavior or proper form of worship. The apostle James puts this in proper perspective by saying that faith divorced from deeds is lifeless (James 2:17). Paul warns against the doctrines of men as having an appearance of wisdom in self- imposed religion, and false humility," (Colossians 2:23).

> *"If anyone among you thinks he is religious, and does not bridle his tongue but deceives his own heart, this ones religion is useless. Pure and undefiled religion before God and the Father is this: to visit orphans and widows in their trouble, and to keep oneself unspotted from the world,"*

(James 1:26-27).

Even though the Amish are known to be a religious people committed to the traditions of men, they are much more than that, many have become an extension of Jesus to many people and in many forms by their charitable giving to each other, their fellowman, and to the world at large. They minister to each other as they are lead by the Holy Spirit and express the love of Christ to each other in many diversified ways.

When national tragedies occur such as tornados or hurricanes they are first responders on location giving of their time to rebuild. They have their own health insurance and when their neighbors experience the loss of life or property they react in the most authentic Jesus kind of way. If a barn burns down, in several days a new one stands in its place as a testimony of the goodness and kindness of their heart. They have their own mental health facility staffed by their people including a support group for counseling and prayer and have had a voice in Washington by their appointed Amish representatives to voice their convictions and concerns.

When there is a death they support not only each other as they gather together for a time of grieving, but also have their gentle way of expressing their support many times in a non-verbal communication that becomes more powerful than words.

My youngest brother Isaac works for the funeral director and says it is not uncommon for the grieving family to never receive the expenses of the funeral which had been paid for by a fellowman. Their spirit of forgiveness was revealed to the world through the tragedy of what has become known as, "The School House Massacres."

Forgiveness is a way of life for the Amish; this has become a part of who they are. We were taught to always be honest, to love our neighbors, not self seeking but to always live for the good of others.

In his senor years Dad was employed at a local Planning Mill. To provide coffee for his fellow workers was his way of reaching out to the men he worked with; they expressed their gratitude by donating their quarters in a coffee can. Years following his retirement a fellow employer stop by for a visit, Dad told how the man had aged and how he hardly recognized him. "I came to make things right with you and ask for your forgiveness," the man said. Dad had no idea what he was referring too.

"During the years I took many quarters from your coffee can and have no idea how much the amount would be, but I want to repay you. Now the man is weeping saying, "I have not slept well for a long time." Dad's response was, "Have you told the Lord about this?" the man said, "Yes! Many times, but I have no peace in my soul. I want to make this right with you, just tell me how much I owe you and I will gladly pay the amount." Dad responded by saying,

"Since you told the Lord about it, and now you told me, we'll consider this as forgiven and forgotten!"

It was in this same spirit that the Holy Spirit would led us as a family to explore new frontiers, working in us, through us, but always for Himself and His divine purpose, which is also now being expressed through our children and our grandchildren, in many diverse forms and geographical locations, and will continue by their devotion and commitment as to what they believe by what they have been taught as our prayers follow them, since they too are being led by the Spirit of God.

Never Limit Your Potential

Nearly forty years have passed since that night in St. Johns Antigua when the Lord confirmed my vision as a child. Why I had limited myself to the black faces of Africa and the Caribbean islands, I'm not sure, but I was about to embark on another missionary adventure unlike anything I had ever experienced, I would be seeing more black faces, but this time in southeast India. I would be introduced to a religious system, a people who worshiped more than three million different gods.

For a number of years my brother Mel had been ministering to the tribal people of India, including the lepers and orphans, the poorest of the poor and the most rejected people in the world. India is a place that my brother was familiar with, he had personally worked with mother Teresa on different occasions and together we would visit several of her institutions.

Mel shared with me how that on one occasion as he entered the kitchen area of an Indian restaurant as he introduced himself to the people who were working there. They said, "Your wife's name is Anna Mary!" He informed them that it was his brother that they had been listening to on the radio including Anna Mary's children's story-time program. Little did I realize that some day I would personally meet these same people in that same restaurant!

The amazing thing about this is, our broadcasts were recorded in our studio in northeast Tennessee and transmitted from an island in the West Indies and carried over the Atlantic Ocean on the airwaves to south east India and heard in a primitive street-side restaurant, some of these listeners having no concept of who Jesus Christ wants to be for them.

Numerous institutions and ministries are doing their best with what they have to assist with a desperate situation bringing hope to human suffering presenting the gospel of Jesus Christ. To see individuals stricken with leprosy eating without hands, with open soars, walking with only stubs for feet yet having a smile on their face is overwhelming to say the least.

Leprosy eats away at the human flesh leaving its victims without feelings or hope, desperation is reflected in their faces, their heart cries out for hope and all their emotions respond to the slightest love and care anyone offers.

Sin also is a type of leprosy that eats away at the soul of the individual living in sin and unbelief without Christ in their heart has made these people some of the most desperate, sin ravaged and deprived poverty stricken people on the earth, this is why so many people are moved with compassion to help by becoming an extension of Jesus bringing hope into hopeless situations as they are being lead and provided for by the Holy Spirit.

Dad and Mom had already made a substantial contribution to the needs of these poor people. Mother had made countless quilts and blankets to keep them warm during their cold nights with many people sleeping by the side of a road. I was greatly moved when I saw a blanket that Mother made covering a person whose only place to live was the side of a dirty street. Together Dad and Mom invested in the needs of one of the orphanages, one of my sacred moments was to witness and to also take a photo of the memorial dedicated to my Dad in his honor on the grounds of the garden area of the orphanage.

Eyes Are the Window of the Soul

When an elderly lady tried to communicate with me I could not understand her language, but I saw into her soul as I witnessed the hurt in her eyes. My interpreter informed me that she was explaining how she has been taking care of her four grandchildren which surrounded her and all they had to eat was third grade rice, that being the same as the cattle were eating. I couldn't help but to think about our grandchildren and the love we have for them and how I would be willing to even die for them if need be, this grandmother was no different. What a thrill it was to share with the grandmother financial blessings from my Sunday school class who had provided me with sufficient funds for just such an occasion, the smile on her face assured me of her gratitude.

To enter into satan's domain is treading on dangerous ground unless we pray that the Holy Spirit would cause our feet to walk upon holy ground. The first thing my brother and I did as we entered the country was to kneel and claim the very ground we walked upon for Jesus Christ, praying for His protection to lead us and keep us from danger. His protection became obvious as we continued on our mission.

My purpose in accompanying my brother was to teach and train the tribal pastors. My first attack from the enemy was to contract a severe sore throat; I could hardly talk for almost a week. I was finally taken to a hospital miles from where we wanted to serve where they gave me penicillin which soon remedied my situation.

The tribal region of southeast India could be compared to a paradise with numerous coffee, sugar, and rice plantations. The vegetation, tropical flowers and numerous waterfalls all add to the splendor of the region, yet the people are very poor.

Following several weeks of ministry in the tribal area which was five thousand feet above the plains area, we were scheduled to travel south about a days journey to conduct a pastor's conference. Monsoon rains had pledged the area from the day we had arrived. On the morning of our departure, our taxi driver informed us of our apparent delay since a tree had fallen across the hairpin road leading down into the valley; we had now been delayed by exactly one hour as we made our way down into the valley.

As we traveled, we noticed the water continued to rise and many areas were now completely flooded. We had crossed several bridges that were quite long and noticed the people that were lined on both sides of the bridge, but we did not realize they had moved to higher ground since their homes had been washed away by the flood water.

By this time we were pushing water with the jeep which came up to the dash board and the traffic came to a complete stop. Our driver asked a passer-by why we were being delayed, his response was that the bridge one hour down the road had washed away and many people had perished; now we knew why we had been delayed by one hour. We also understood why the Indian pastor who had stayed with us at our hotel informed us that during the night he had a vision and saw five larger than life angels standing around our beds with swords drawn in protection.

Our driver turned the vehicle toward the side of the road and drove into the field, we finally came to higher ground and followed a cow-path which led us to a gravel road and finally back to the main road.

Unrealized to us was that protestors had convened on the conference hall before our arrival which had now all been cleared away by the time we arrived. The following day Mel and I ministered to the pastors for an all day event including providing them with a traditional meal of rice served on banana leaves with funds provided by my Sunday school class; we also presented all the sixty pastors present with a new white shirt and the forty ladies with new dresses.

Our mission trip to India was cut short when we learned that our only sister, Ruth, and the only one of our family that remained with the Amish was stricken with an aneurism of the brain. The word we received was they were considering taking her off the life support system; this meant that we would have to leave immediately to be home in time for her funeral. Our travel time back to Dulles took a total of thirty six hours. We had called home from Germany when we changed flights and were informed that Ruth was still alive. Family and friends had met at the hospital and prayed around the clock and even had services in the visitors lounge at the hospital where total strangers joined in the prayer time and the singing.

Together as a family we were to witness another miracle of God's amazing grace when our sister opened her eyes and asked for her husband Leroy. Her twin daughters who were praying and also pleading with their mother to not leave them, assuring her that they loved and still needed her. What a thrill it was to hear Ruth say several minutes after we had prayer, "You came back from India to see me!" Her recovery process has been astounding and time has been a wonderful healer as we slowly witnessed the Lords amazing healing grace.

Time has been a wonderful healer for many of God's people who have discovered Him in their extreme moments of helplessness and pain when all seemed lost only to witness His mighty supernatural power breaking through our impossible situations to confirm Himself as our healer for all our sicknesses and diseases.

No matter what we encounter in life all things are possible for us who believe, it may not always work out as we hoped for, but we are committed to the will and mercy of God and are resigned to His perfect will.

It is during moments like this that we hear Him speak into our spirit, to learn to know the voice of God as He communicates with us by the Holy Spirit, should not be difficult for us to understand since Jesus said, *"My sheep know My voice."*

To distinguish between our humanness and selfish ambitions, to know and hear His voice requires our spiritual discernment which is always discovered through prayer, fasting and waiting before Him.

I was certain that I heard His voice when He informed me that I was to purchase a guitar for someone in India. When I informed one of my friends about my decision, he immediately volunteered to provide the gift. Not knowing how to transport such a valuable instrument I decided to make a nice cherry box with brass hardware. My brother informed me that we should disguise the box during transport so that it's not stolen; however, since we had prayed and dedicated the guitar as a Sunday school class, I said, "the Lord will take care of it." Little did we realize how true that statement would become upon our arrival; all our luggage came down the carousel but the cherry box with the guitar inside, all we could do now was to file a lost claim with the airlines and continue to our hotel.

Why we were detained as we taxied away from the terminal toward the runway in Germany for our final flight to India we were not sure, all we remembered was the voice on the intercom saying that there was a suspicious package on board and we would be detained until it was removed, the only thing to do now was to pray, so we prayed! "Lord the box with the guitar belongs to you, if someone stole it have them return it, if its lost please find it and we pray that it would be delivered right here on this very spot." Why we were so specific I'm not sure, but that is exactly what happened, later that night the call from Germany interrupted our sleep to inform us that the box had been located and would be delivered to this address the next day around 9:00 am. The delivery man could not speak English as he entered the room, even though, unrealized, all he knew to do was to be obedient to the Holy Spirit and set the box on the very spot were Mel and I had prayed.

Not until we entered the tribal pastors home and met his twenty one year old daughter Mercy, were we made aware that she was praying for just such a guitar and when she began playing and singing, "Lord I lift Your name on high, Lord I love to sing Your praises," we knew that the Lord had fulfilled her request. Today, Mercy is involved in tribal ministries and we are told that wherever she goes that guitar becomes her tool for evangelism.

The highlight of my trip to India was to fulfill the request for a tribal House of Prayer. For twenty five years pastor Abraham had been praying for a place to conduct services. Following his conversion twenty five years earlier, his wife had left him since she did not wish to convert to Christianity, now we are placing the cornerstones for the proposed building on his land.

When Mel invited me to accompany him to India, I informed my Sunday school class that four thousand dollars would build a House of Prayer, many of the class members responded in a number of ways and we had sufficient funds for the project. Today there is a stone building erected and built by the people of the community as a testimony of God's love in a population of twenty thousand people who do not know the Lord.

The greatest miracle concerning the house of prayer is when pastor Abraham's wife Sarah heard that the God her husband was praying to had heard his twenty five year prayer, and since the god she had prayed to never did anything for her she decided that she wants to return to her husband Abraham, to be a faithful wife and to also become a born-again Christian.

Today pastor Abraham and his wife Sarah are faithfully serving the Lord in their new building provided for by individuals who felt led to respond to the voice of the Holy Spirit, even though they are experiencing severe opposition to the gospel with several members recently being brutally attacked by those opposing the gospel.

Our Lives are Scheduled Assignments

Have you ever wondered why you are going through all the various experiences in your life, why certain things happen and why you meet new people, total strangers that become you're good friends. You find yourself traveling to areas you didn't know existed and out of that things develop that you never thought possible. We forget to comprehend the fact that as God's people we are on assignment for Him. That might mean doing things we don't even like to do or it might involve the fulfillment of our highest aspirations. We have our life-time to accomplish for God what we were designed to become, life is a development of everything we are about, everything about us changes, with each new day we grow older and the years add up before we realize what happened and we are heading for our eternity. We will meet the Lord someday, because this too is on His schedule for us, someday we will leave this world via the grave, or when He comes in clouds of glory to receive us unto Himself, either way we will go to our assigned destiny.

Faith plays a major role of our spiritual development since, *"Without faith it is impossible to please God,"* our life is meant and designed to be a walk of faith; a faith forward action, step by step, person by person adventure of anointed service for God's glory. When we walk in step with the Lord we will realize that our down time is just as productive as our fruit bearing season. The Christian life is compared to as a tree planted by a water stream that brings forth its fruit in its season, [See Psalms 1.]

The origin and the life of the fruit bearing are because of the deep root system that has developed over time and is connected to the water source. In this case, the Water of life, Jesus Christ, and by the indwelling power of the Holy Spirit, the tree is never independent from that water supply, and the fruit always develops from the life in the branches of the tree. First, there is evidence of life coming forth from the branches which soon develops into buds, followed by blooms. The evidence of life is in the fruit according to the nature and species of the tree. However, to prepare for next years crop the tree becomes dormant for a season so that it might again bear fruit also for a season otherwise it would burn out and die.

This is a good analogy to describe what is going on with our lives and how the Lord will use us for His purpose and glory as we are lead by His Spirit. As we reflect on our past to evaluate where we have been and how the Lord leads us to accomplish our various assignments, we cannot help but to be amazed and marvel at His goodness and to also have the attitude of the tree planted which never boasts about its accomplishments, even though it shares its bounties and shares its story as it continues to bloom and bear fruit and when it becomes dormant again it never complains that there are no signs of anything happening, the tree doesn't even understand its own nature, it just responds to its supernatural life source.

Chapter Eleven

On Assignment for God

A s we grow together in Christ by allowing God's Word to fill and enrich our spirit we become conformed together as the body of Christ in a unity of purpose. Only as we learn together what the Lord desires to do in each one of us together, will we be able to grow into full maturity impacting the world overflowing as a river.

For God's Word to effectively communicate into our spirit, there are several things we must be aware of. First we must pray that the Holy Spirit would communicate "God's truth" into our spirit and second we must block all distractions or we will miss the communication of the Spirit to edify our spirit. This is more important then we might realize; to miss this communication is to miss hearing from God; therefore, we will not be able to communicate His message to His world. My writing may be inspired and anointed by the Holy Spirit but that will never take the place of God's inspired Holy Word to nurture the soul.

The unity of any group of people growing together always nurtures their spiritual strength. This must be of great importance if we expect to grow together because our unity becomes our source for spiritual effectiveness as a witness for Christ.

As Christians in the world today, we are the body of Christ, "Called out" by the Holy Spirit to build the Kingdom of Christ on earth.

The body of Christ must always be on guard, what is it that binds us together, or what is it that pulls us apart? Love always serves as the binding agent, the adhesive that holds a body of believers together.

When love grows cold, anything can happen that may cause the greatest fire-storm any body of believers could imagine and it always gives place to the enemy. There is no greater damage to the body of Christ than a disruption of peace when love grows cold for one another. What are some of the safe-guards we can examine to work at maintaining a peaceful harmonious worshipful atmosphere and spiritually healthy body of Christ?

When individuals allow their emotions to come between themselves and their fellowman anything can erupt, when there is mutual respect for leadership and fellowman, living with a godly fear any group of people are always greatly empowered.

Truth and love are the two most powerful attributes in the home and in the body of Christ including the world, when these two attributes find their spiritual growth from the Word of God in prayer for one another; we can have a foretaste of heaven on earth.

When a body of believers becomes unified it becomes almost impossible for the enemy to drive his wedge between personalities and rather than being defeated, they become stronger in commitment, faith and life.

When truth and love are in place as knitted together as a strong cord this will result in a powerful binding relationship that is not easily severed. When the cords of love become interwoven into the fabric of our lives, God's Kingdom always comes to earth and His will is accomplished since it is God's will for us that we live in unity, harmony and love.

As Christians, many of us have experienced church at its best and at its worst state of being, but we don't live there, we only learn from our mistakes to not repeat them, and we move on with our lives. God's will for our individual lives is to make our faith journey pleasant and enjoyable, even delightful, to make our contribution memorable.

Unity is our Strength

We should be the happiest, most jubilant victorious people on the earth. Before we can live together as a unified body we have to confess and put behind us all grievances and animosities that have hindered our past.

When individuals choose to live together in the atmosphere and attitude of forgiveness they can conquer anything. Forgiveness conditions the soil of our lives to sow love seeds into the lives of each other which will result in spiritual prosperity with an eternal harvest.

People who struggle with unforgiveness do not possess God's peace but rather live in turmoil of soul, mind and spirit. What is even more tragic, when they talk about it they most often talk to the wrong people and never mention it to the Lord who is their only help in their time of need. The only way for anyone to experience peace with their fellowman is to talk about it to those who care enough to help them to discover restoration and forgiveness, this always means we must take the initiative to either call their number, write a letter, make a visit, say I'm sorry, "I forgive!" or whatever it takes to bring resolve. I have seen individuals lose there health, grow old before their time and go to an early grave all because they harbored unforgiveness.

Kingdom people always grow together and are always thinking about seed time and harvest, eternal investments. When the soil of their lives are well watered by the Word it is amazing how soon a seed will germinate and spring forth with growth to soon bear a bountiful harvest.

For this to mature everyday must begin with time spent in prayer not only for direction for the day, but for those we share our lives with. This becomes our most sacred and best moments of our day with the Lord. To refuse God's best for our day is to a great loss to miss. To take our talents with us to the grave is a great eternal loss; the only way God meant for us to leave this world is to be completely emptied of self, and filled with His resurrection power. Millions die without ever discovering their best gifts, to never lay up treasure in heaven, to come before the Lord empty handed, simply means we never invested our lives and talents for His glory. When a person dies, our earthly potential dies with us; many never knew they had spiritual gifts because they had never discovered the Lord. Others thought the task was to large they simply did nothing when all we are meant to do is to influence one person at a time as we live our lives day by day.

Included in our prayer we should ask the Lord who we can invest our life in today, what words or deeds can we bring into action to assist the other person to become all they can be? Thereby becoming what they may never have become had we not involved ourselves in their lives through prayer.

God uses our unique giftedness to expand His Kingdom on the earth. In teaching His disciples how to pray, Jesus instructed them to pray, *"Your Kingdom come Your will be done on earth as in heaven."* Jesus was simply encouraging and instructing the disciples how to live and serve together for His purpose and glory in bringing about His will and purpose concerning His Kingdom.

We can so easy forget that, church, fellowship and witness, everything that church is about, is all about Jesus calling unto Himself a people from out of the world, re-created, born-again, Spirit filled, unified, without spot or wrinkle, and perfected in Him, heaven bound!

In this preparation process it becomes the work of the Holy Spirit by our cooperation to iron out those wrinkles and allow Jesus to keep us by His power and in His love maintaining His peace in our heart among our fellowman.

To grow together gracefully and spiritually the body of Christ must do everything in reference to Jesus Christ as the head of the body. There are many sad commentaries of real life situations when daily patience, meekness, charitableness and forgiveness were not in place and the results are always devastating and divisive, especially when individuals try to live in both worlds of the flesh and the Spirit.

We have a wrong concept of life if we think we can live in both worlds of flesh and Spirit. Unless we deny the world, the flesh and the devil, we can easily give place to the enemy, and we mess up our life.

Fighting's and war among the people of God is not from God, they come from out of the natural world from which we were delivered. Our human nature has a fighting instinct; there are people who love to stir up strife, when estrangements happen it sometimes takes years to resolve, leaving bitter scars. When God's people live in an atmosphere of redemptive relationships they can conquer every demon that comes their way and they bring God's Kingdom to this earth.

History provides us with the story of failure and redemption beginning with the first book of the Bible and the story unfolds through the century's right into our day. Fire-storms are not uncommon and they have left a blazing trail of devastation that has scared many lives, and destroyed many great men and women of God.

When love is absent and indifference takes over it is like a plague turning an atmosphere into a hellish nightmare and there are many losses, with absolutely nothing gained.

I know, because I have lived through some of the worst of this in my pastoral experience. Since no two people seldom see things the same way, with a difference of opinion, or the interpretation of scripture, church fellowship becomes a great challenge and can be one of the most peaceful harmonious experiences we can have as a body of Christ here on the earth, but we all have an obligation to maintain our peace to make our fellowship work. If we could always work toward building each other up in faith, what would church be like if our judgments of each other were only redemptive? If we would purpose in our heart to never cause the other person to feel inferior, to guard our speech and realize that silence is gold.

As the body of Christ, we operate by spiritual laws, the law of life and growth are already in us, by the *"law of the Spirit of Life in Christ Jesus"* operating in us we can not remain the same, we either grow more spiritual with increasing faith experience and knowledge, becoming wiser, or we deteriorate becoming indifferent critical and bitter.

People are always the problem, but people can also be the solution, one person can create by their presence a wholesome atmosphere among a thousand people simply by their unity of oneness and spirit, while another person can create just the opposite. How many times have you witnessed a person walking into a room filled with people and the atmosphere took on a holy atmosphere? This same principle applies to a negative situation as well.

One of the greatest hindrances to spiritual growth is to fall into a pattern of routine, when there is no Holy Spirit presence and everything becomes mechanical, someone once said, "If the Holy Spirit would be removed from the average congregation everything would operate the same." This is indeed a sad commentary but true.

We Are New Creations

As a body of believers we are also a community of believers, our spiritual influence, our consistency, our self control, our victory over the flesh puts us in right position to be God's people in our world today. When we esteem each other higher than self, when our life-light shines into darkness, when souls are brought into the Kingdom, when faith increases, when the Holy Sprit is present, when we discover ourselves aging together, sharing our cookies and coffee with each other, all this has greater merit than we can ever imagine and God is well pleased.

God has given gifts to man for the purpose of training, to disciple, and for the development of faith and character, to grow together in the grace and knowledge of Christ, to influence one another by the way we live out our faith and how we share that faith together.

Our commission from Christ is to teach, preach and make disciples. We have majored in both teaching and preaching, but we have lagged behind in disciplining people; to disciple a person means we have to spend time with them as new born and immature babies in Christ. To disciple people takes lots of precious time, it means we have to hold them in our arms as new born babies. We all know what happens as we feed a new born baby, just when we think they are accepting what we place in their mouth they decide to throw-up on us and at the same time they make a mess on our lap and we have to change their diaper.

This is what we don't like, and this is why we shy away from becoming so personally involved with people. It simply requires more that we are willing to do, but this is how people grow together, through love and tender caring, a good feeding and nourishing program, even cleaning up the mess. If you don't understand what I'm trying to say it is obvious you have never been in such a situation.

Changing the Course of History

Since we have a world of people living all around us where can we begin to win our world for Christ, and how is the best way for us to serve them, since many people we know already profess to belong to the body of Christ. How can we make a significant difference in such a diverse community of individuals? How can we make an impact for Christ's Kingdom and can we really change the course of history?

The disciples all made their contribution in doing just that. Is this possible for us today? When the apostle Paul was converted, he not only changed the course of history, he impacted eternity, both the kingdom of darkness and the Kingdom of light, and we too, have our call of God to introduce Jesus to our world.

The writers of the four gospels, Matthew, Mark, Luke and John changed the course of history by impacting the kingdom of darkness and winning many sons and daughters into glory. At one time these men were not Christians—Matthew for example, was a tax collector, thought of as the scum beneath the scum since he defrauded people. But the power of the gospel changed him and he brought change to history, he too impacted the world of darkness and the Kingdom of Light. This becomes our challenge to serve our world for Christ today. We can impact history; we have just one lifetime to do that.

There is absolutely no greater joy than to lead a person to Christ, to witness the transforming power of the gospel, to lend a hand to a fellow traveler, to bring joy to the world and offer words of encouragement which is the greatest ministry of all time.

In the great commission, Jesus told the disciples to go to the entire world, this meant they should witness for Christ as they were going, one day at a time, and one soul at a time, the same applies for us today. Service opportunities are everywhere, while we are in flight to some far away place sitting beside a stranger or at the local hardware store.

While waiting to check out one day out of habit I asked the older lady how her day was going, I noticed a tear in her eye and she looked sad, I asked her if she wanted to talk about it, she responded by saying, "Do you see that man going out the door, he just spoke very unkind words to me and he's a pastor."

I asked if I could pray for her, she nodded yes. I did the same thing to another checkout person a year later at the same counter, "How's your day going?" She smiled and affirmed that all was well. I shared my story concerning the older Lady, "O! I heard about that, she told me about someone praying with her, but now she's gone."

Seeing Through Our Fathers Eyes

Jesus is still recruiting individuals today from all walks of life, from every background and culture, the task is not complete the fields of the world are ripe for harvest. Is it possible for us today to grasp the scope of our mission to tell the world, to go and serve our fellowman in the name of Jesus, to share with our world the deep utterance of God expressed through His One and only Son Jesus Christ? Not until we see through our Fathers eyes and with His heart of compassion revealed in us can we truly comprehend the urgency of this moment in time that can change and impact eternity.

Where do we begin, what shall we continue, what should we eliminate, who should we involve and recruit? Jesus began His ministry with twelve men, the witness spread into neighboring countries and finally around the world. But millions still have not heard, so how can we make an impact that will contribute to the cause? Just imagine yourself writing a letter, you are entering into your journal the happenings as you witnessed them, but little do you realize that your letter might some day be printed and circulated around the world for millions to read.

This is exactly what happened to the disciples. Their letters were first written on parchment what had been verbalized for years including their own personal encounters and as eyewitness of having walked and served with Jesus on this earth.

Much later their letters were circulated through primitive printing presses, and then modern presses becoming the most widely distributed book in the entire world, the Bible. They had absolutely no idea how they would go and serve in Christ's name and who all or how many people would become inspired by their writings, millions of preachers and lay people have drawn from the well of their inspiration. This will continue as long as time lasts making the biggest impact on the world concerning the greatest story ever told.

The Great Commission is meant to plant faith seeds in the lives of people. Jesus had much to say about soil conditions, there is hard ground; rocky ground, good ground, and battle ground. Out of millions who went to their grave and never learned to know Jesus is a great tragedy, but there is a remnant of people who decided they will take God at His Word; they chose to believe and become obedient followers as His witnesses, many becoming martyrs of the faith.

The story of God and humanity unfolds like a curtain across the stage of time and at the center of all the activity, we see a form appearing, the life and light of the Son of God reaching out to His world through people like you and me building His Kingdom, a Bride for His glory to inhabit His eternity and sharing that with, *"Whosoever will may come."*

God at times paints with a broad brush stroke and sometimes with fine detail, yet all according to His will and purpose. He has been grateful and merciful with men and nations allowing them to choose to make mistakes giving them time to repent, giving them His permission to decide their own eternal destiny.

It is important for us to seize our moments of opportunity; we live in a day when the world is knocking on our door. How do you respond to a telemarketer calling you at an inconvenient moment? Rather than just rudely hanging up, I decided to accept the challenge, the voice on the other end of the line said, I needed their credit card and I responded by saying I don't need credit. Now the voice is raised in response by saying, "Everyone in America needs credit today!" I responded by saying, "But I'm different, my Father is very wealthy and He said everything that is His I have a right to all His wealth." After the pause, my friend asked, "What does your father do?" I said, "He's in the cattle business, He owns cattle on every hill all over the world and He even wrote a book about Himself that has become the best seller and is printed in every language of the world, would you like for me to read a portion of His writings?" Now rather than me hanging up on the caller, the caller hangs up on me. Maybe this is not the most tactful approach, but at least I challenged the person in a non-threatening way and gave him food for thought.

The Bible holds no secrets but provides us with an open book to history and prophecy including tactics for evangelism with clear concise teachings about our eternity. As history reveals to us the facts, and prophecy reveals the future, the Bible still provides those with vision and purpose who choose to follow Jesus Christ into His world to gather the harvest when people from all nations will be gathered before Him and the curtain is closed to the preaching of the gospel. "What have we done in our time that will honor His cause to serve Him well?" May we purpose to be a redemptive spiritual force in our world today so others can enjoy His presence in His Kingdom?

Chapter Twelve

When Day is Done

Do you ever wonder what lies beyond the sunset? You find yourself gazing into the far away unknown; you even desire to be there now! You wonder what lies beyond all that expanse of cloud and sky, of universe and you don't have to wonder where God is since you sense His presence everywhere.

With my aspirations as an artist it becomes a natural experience for me to lose myself in the beauty of God's creation. From my viewpoint, I could see the Blue Ridge Mountains to the East and the Allegany Mountains to the West, it was evening time and the day with all its activities was drawing to a close, the curtain was closing upon the day.

Down in the valley I saw several deer grazing by the edge of the woods. I stood there and tried to take in the awesome moment in time. The panoramic view, the cool mountain breeze blowing over my face with God's peace in my soul, Wow! What a moment in time to enjoy one's relationship with the everlasting Lord.

Anna Mary and I had prayed that morning as we always do, we watched the mother dove that had built her nest in a hanging basket beside the patio door to raise her baby's, they

191

were as hungry as we were, but we were even more hungry for God and He was feeding our soul.

Long ago we learned the value of spending time together in prayer with the Lord to help us through our day interceding for our children and those we love, praying that the Holy Spirit would lead us to someone that needed our friendship and encouragement.

Now I'm viewing the sunset as it sets over the western mountains, I am thinking about my eternal home, far away out there in that distant realm. It seems I hear voices of the past, loved ones beckoning me home, I could only imagine the sights and sounds they must be enjoying. Our loved one's that are already there—what are they doing now and what is the present heaven really like? We all have thoughts about the place Jesus went to prepare for us; sometimes we long to be there even now.

Beyond the Sunset

I continued to watch the sun as it was slowly sinking into the night, another day had come and gone, God was splashing His paint brush across the sky with an array of color beauty and wonder that no human artist could imitate.

Someday we will also soar into that great unknown. As Christian's, eternity is already inside of us and we live with a longing to be there now even though we enjoy our life with God on earth.

Our experience and our life with God has taught us that we are not destined to remain on this earth, His Word informs us of His eternal rest for us that awaits our arrival, that we are only passing through this world to be a witness for Him, to reveal His love to our world as an extension of who He is and of all He desires to be in us, in the world today.

The spectacle before me witnessed to me that since the beginning of time and from eternity past, God is still the same and that He was revealing Himself to me now, again! That we are the one's that are being changed into His image more and more to one day be like Him and to see Him as He is. That the same fire that hovered over the tents of the children of Israel so long ago is that same fire that we feel burning within our soul now! It is the presence of the Holy Spirit assuring us that all is well, that God's promises will not fail and one day heaven will be a reality for all those who accepted Jesus Christ as their personal Savior.

Night had slowly crept in, the stars were lighting up the sky, the sunset was lost to the darkness, but I also realized that beyond the sunset there were more clouds, sky and space, that the sun was still shining somewhere and the everlasting God was present everywhere, that He is with us by His Spirit to embrace us with His peace and that I was not the only one admiring His beauty, somewhere in the wide world of people, someone was also praising His name for the beauty of who He is.

In our fleeting moments in time all He desires to do is to reveal Himself to us by His peace and love, preparing us for that moment in time when we soar into the great eternity. Someday in eternity we will be able to see the other side of the sunset when day is done; there will be no need for the sun, since Jesus will be the light shining forever. The night will fade away with the dawning of the new day when the Son of righteousness appears with healing in His wings.

In this life God shares Himself with us for who He is, and what He desires to do in us to prepare us for eternity with Him, to be washed by His blood and cleansed from our sins, the apostle Paul gives us this hope in God.

"But we all, with unveiled face, beholding as in a mirror the glory of the Lord, are being transformed

into the same image from glory to glory, just as by the Spirit of the Lord,"

(2 Corinthians 3:18).

"Beloved, now are we the children of God; and it has not yet been revealed what we shall be, but we know that when He is revealed, we shall be like Him, for we shall see Him as He is,"

(1 John 2:3).

In this life God allows us to see just enough of Himself to draw us and to secure us into Himself. This was His purpose for sending Jesus into the world to be our peace by the indwelling presence of the Holy Spirit.

He made His presence known to Moses and the Children of Israel through the Ark of the Covenant. Inside the sacred Golden box were the Ten Commandments, the manna or bread, and Aarons Rod that budded, on top of the Ark were the two angels bowed in worship.

Inside the believer is God's law *"hidden within our heart."* Within the believer is Jesus," *The Bread of Life."* Aarons Rod that budded meant that he was a chosen vessel of God, we are *"His chosen people,"* we are *"His royal priesthood,"* we are *"the people of God, a holy nation"* in the world today. *"The angels of the Lord encamp around about them that fear Him."* We carry God's presence within our spirit.

Since God is totally completely altogether peace, we should be no less peaceful individuals, Jesus said, *"Blessed are the peacemakers,"* we must appropriate His peace in our "right now" moments of uncertainty and speak peace words over our life and situations.

No one was allowed to touch the Ark, only the Levites were allowed to carry it, only those persons who are *"born again"* are allowed to carry the presence of Jesus, to touch the Ark meant certain death and this is why I mentioned earlier, be careful who touches your life!

Experiencing our Soul

We experience an inner working of the Holy Spirit in our soul, we experience God's peace, the freedom of deliverance, our soul desires to magnify the Lord, to experience something of eternity while we live in this world in our natural body of flesh, our soul is the only part of our being that will never die, our old body of flesh will be resurrected becoming a glorified body should we go by way of the grave, or if we are caught up with the Lord when He comes in the rapture we will be changed in a moment to have a glorified body in heaven, this will be our final victory.

God allows us to see just enough of who He is to secure us in Himself. He allows those special moments in time to capture our attention to sense an awareness of His greatness so that we might experience His Holy Spirit in our soul.

This is why the Holy Spirit indwells our lives with His presence, revealing a dimension of Himself that only He can provide.

In heaven, our soul will have a glorified body, free from pain sickness and death. To experience our soul is to know the condemnation that sin brings to our conscience, including the guilt it produces as a result of our disobedience and the freedom Jesus Christ provides when we become surrendered to His Lordship as we receive His forgiveness.

Becoming Complete in Christ

Life is not a funny, funny riddle, life is a revelation, the secrets of our inner-most being and our destiny are revealed to us in the person of Jesus Christ, and this is why we will never really know who we actually are until we discover ourselves in a salvation experience in Jesus Christ.

Jesus Christ stands before the easel of our life and with one hand He reaches into heaven securing our eternity and with the other hand He paints a beautiful picture of our redemption on earth.

While on earth, His hands reached out to humanity who felt His healing touch, hands that had healed multitudes were now tortured with the pain of death on a cross to bring completion to our redemption, so when the sun of our life goes down we have an eternal dwelling place in God's heaven.

The Bible gives us a descriptive view of that eternal dwelling place of the soul by saying, *"In My Father's house are many mansions,"* Including innumerable numbers of heavenly hosts, loved ones who have already entered there and are waiting to greet us and welcome us into the company of the redeemed.

God's entire purpose for us is to prepare us for that moment in time when we will be transported into eternity.

The moment in time that I experienced as I watched the sun set was not only what I beheld with my natural eyes, but what I saw with my spiritual eyes, the awesome presence of His purity, how His cleansing power within us captivates our lives conforming us into His image, we are the crowning act of all His creativity through Jesus Christ.

Just as this day now faded into the sunset was special to Him to never again repeat itself. His mercies are being renewed every morning with each new day, and so are we as His people living each day with renewed strength, and new revelations of who He desires to be in us while we represent Him in this world.

A Sure Guarantee

God keeps an accurate account of every person born into the world including their individual deeds and words. He knows the thoughts of mankind afar off. He knows those who are His and He welcomes those who reject him; Jesus Christ is man's final judge and will have the last Word involving everything.

We must never judge anyone, not by the way they lived, or the way they died. There are many testimonies of individuals who came to know the Lord in the final moments of their lives; I have personally stood by their death bed as they received Jesus Christ into their heart.

The people who had known them for who they were and how they lived their lives no doubt thought of them as having missed heaven. The death of a soul that dies without Jesus Christ or the hope of eternal life is the greatest tragedy to befall any individual. For one's soul to pass over the great divide to never be able to return to their former state of being, to be forever severed and separated without hope in God, to never know the joy of heaven or all that Jesus had personally prepared for them and would have been there upon their arrival to enjoy in a world without end is most tragic indeed.

My question is, had they never heard, did they not care, or did they not understand? I personally believe that more people will miss heaven simply because they did not fully understand the message and as a result of this they never really knew how to commit their lives to the Lord.

Every Word about God for us is a sure guarantee, our birth guarantees our death, and our death guarantees our appearing before our maker which guarantees our day of judgment, a day of celebration and of rewarding or of great regret!

The blood of Jesus secures our forgiveness and our confession of faith agrees that Jesus Christ secured our salvation on the cross. Rejection of Christ guarantees spiritual death, death cannot destroy the soul, the person that dies without Jesus Christ will live forever without life, where the soul never dies and survives only to suffer, to be cut off from its highest destiny and driven from the only one who had already provided resurrection and eternal life.

Heaven, a City in Preparation

The final drama of this present world as we know it referred to in scripture as *"the end of the age"* the curtain falls upon the stage of time, and eternity continues, this present dispensation as we knew it has ended, *"When Day is Done"* and Jesus now reigns eternally as "King of Kings and Lord of Lords," The old earth that was cursed as a result of Adams transgression has passed away.

By that same power that God spoke the world into being we will witness the Lord Jesus Christ speak into being the New Earth and the New Heaven, the New Jerusalem prepared as a bride adorned for her husband.

> *"Then I John saw the holy city, New Jerusalem, coming down out of heaven from God, prepared as a bride adorned for her husband. And I heard a loud voice from heaven saying, "Behold," the tabernacle of God is with men, and He will dwell with them, and they shall be His people. God Himself will be with them and be their God. And God will wipe away every tear from their eyes; there shall be no more death, nor sorrow, nor crying, There shall be no more pain, for the former things have passed away,"*

(Revelation 21:2-4).

Chapter Thirteen

The Coming Prince of Peace

A Brief Overview

At His first coming Jesus came as a baby born in a manger, the angel announced *"Peace on earth good will toward men"* Jesus fulfilled His mission to the earth by paying for the sins of the world and dying on a cross. He rose by His own power and ascended back into heaven to be at the right hand of the Father.

One of the greatest events in the history of the world is about to unfold, Jesus is coming again, this time in clouds of glory, the heavens will part as a scroll, the trump of God will sound and the dead in Christ will resurrect from their graves, and the Christians that are alive and remain will suddenly be caught up together with them in the clouds, so shall we ever be with the Lord.

"Behold I show you a mystery; we shall not all sleep, but we shall all be changed -in a moment, in the twinkling of an eye, at the last trumpet. For the trumpet

shall sound, and the dead shall be raised incorruptible, and we shall be changed,"

(1 Corinthians 15:51-52).

The New Testament gives over 300 references concerning the return of Jesus Christ for His bride, the Church. Jesus is coming to catch away His bride, the Universal body of believers who have been redeemed, those people who in their life accepted Jesus into their heart and remained in a right relationship with Him.

Immediately following this event the seven year "Great Tribulation" will take place on the earth, three and one half years into this period the Antichrist will force upon individuals his mark, known as "the mark of the beast" when people will not be able to buy or sell without taking that mark.

At the end of the seven year period the armies will gather together for battle, the Kings of the east will come, (see Revelation16:12). Two hundred million strong will march to battle on that great day of the Almighty God. (vv.13-14). There aim will be to destroy Israel once and for all. God will come to Israel's rescue and they will finally recognize Jesus as their long awaited Messiah.

His feet shall stand Again on the Mount of Olives

At the end of the seven year period, Jesus will ride out of heaven on a white horse as KING of KINGS and LORD of LORDS, the armies of heaven will follow Him dressed in white, the army includes the redeemed of God, those who had there robes washed in the blood of the Lamb.

Jesus Christ will at this time subdue all His enemies and all evil forces. The Antichrist (beast) and the false prophet will be cast into the lake of fire (Revelation 19:20).

The armies following the Antichrist will be destroyed by the Lord Jesus Christ and His heavenly army, (Revelation 19:11-16).

Satan will be sealed in the bottomless pit for a period of 1000 years, (Revelation 20:1-3). A great battle ensues and Jesus on His white horse with His Word coming out of His mouth destroys all the ungodly Christ rejecting enemies who all perish at the sound of His Word.

The Thousand Year Reign

Jesus will set up His earthly Kingdom and the redeemed will reign with Christ for one thousand years on this present earth. During the 1,000 year period, satan will be bound in the bottomless pit so he will not deceive the nations until his short period of release, (Revelation. 20:3, 7-8).

At the end of the thousand year millennium satan will be released from his prison to go out to deceive the nations. God sends fire from heaven and devoured the devil who is cast into the lake of fire where the beast and the false prophet are to be tormented forever with all Christ rejecters and all people who refused to accept Jesus Christ as their personal Savior, (Revelation. 20:10).

The Judgment of the wicked

The faithful martyrs who have died for the cause of Christ during the seven year tribulation period will be resurrected before the millennium. They too will rule with Christ and will be priests of God and Christ, (Revelation 20:4). The unbelieving dead will wait for the second resurrection when they will appear before God at the Great White Throne judgment to hear the verdict, *"Depart from me into everlasting fire,"* (Revelation 20:5).

Following the 1000 millennium reign of Christ, satan will be released for a season and will again resume his work of deceit, (Revelation 20:7-8).

Believers were resurrected a 1000 years before this judgment and their works were judged at the "judgment seat of Christ," (2 Corinthians. 5:10).

The original gives this as "the Bema seat," (Greek). It means a place where Roman athletes were rewarded for having run the race and were crowned for their effort, this will be a time of rewarding, when the saints will cast their crowns at the feet of Jesus as unworthy to receive them.

At the Great White throne judgment the wicked dead will seek a hiding place from the face of the Lord Jesus Christ their judge, but there will be no place to hide.

The dead, small and great will stand before God, their great accomplishments on earth will find no favor with God and all their good charitable deeds will be of no eternal value. The book of life will be opened to show and to prove that their names do not appear there.

The most important aspect of the millennium is the reign of Christ. Peter taught that Christ now "today" rules from the right hand of God, (Acts 2:33-36).

This rule will last until His enemies are made Christ's footstool. *"The Lord said to my Lord, sit at My right hand, till I make Your enemies Your footstool," (Psalm 110:1).*

The prophet Joel saw into the future and makes reference to the establishment of the Millennial Kingdom, "Millennium" (Latin for 1000 years). (See Joel 3:11-21).

After all enemies are destroyed following the judgment of the wicked John said. "

"And I saw the dead small and great stand before God and the books were opened. And another book was opened which is the Book of Life. And the dead were judged according to their works, by the things

that were written in the books. The sea gave up the dead who were in it, and Death and Hades delivered up the dead who were in them. And they were judged, each one According to his work. Then Death and Hades were cast into the lake of fire. This is the second death. And anyone not found written in the Book of Life was cast into the lake of fire,"

(Revelation 20: 11-15).

Heaven, the New Jerusalem Comes to the New Earth

This is what we have been waiting for, to see the beautiful New Jerusalem coming down from God out of heaven, the restoration of the Garden of Eden.

When man sinned in the Garden of Eden, the earth and the atmospheric heaven came under the curse of sin. Satan became the "god of this age"- this world system, (2 Corinthians 4:4).

When satan is cast into the lake of fire, along with the antichrist and the false prophet, then Christ the creator will recreate the atmospheric heaven, as well as the earth. Peter saw the "Day of the Lord" coming as a thief in the night when the heavens will pass away with a great noise, and the elements will melt with fervent heat; both the earth and the works that are therein will be burned up. He encourages the believer to remain steadfast, blameless, longsuffering and faithful growing in grace and knowledge of the Lord Jesus Christ. (See 2 Peter 3:10-18).

Now our long awaited glimpse into the New Jerusalem will finally arrive; Heaven on this earth, the "New Earth." Wherein dwells righteousness.

John witnessed the unfolding events in Revelation (21:1-27). He provides us with a detailed descriptive overview of the New Jerusalem. No more tears, no pain, former things will have passed away, all manner of precious stones, streets of gold, awesome music and song, glory, praise and worship everywhere, the city itself 1500 miles long, wide and high. There is no need for the sun since Jesus Himself is the light thereof.

The Final Invitation

The day is coming when there will be no more invitations to come to Christ, it will be forever too late! Before the last book of the Bible will come to a close it is as if God said to John, give the invitation one more time, so John said.

"And the Spirit and the bride say, "Come!" And let him who hears say come. Whosoever desires. Let him take the water of life freely,"

(Revelation 22:17).

Information source, The Bible, and New Illustrated Bible Dictionary. Thomas Nelson Publisher

At the end of this book you will find my prayer of invitation, if you are not born again and want to become a Christian please say the words of the prayer with a sincere heart and God will hear and answer your prayer, the prayer is already anointed by the Holy Spirit and you will feel Him as He enters your heart, call me and let me know your decision and I will help you in anyway I can.

Chapter Fourteen

God's City of Gold

Our ultimate goal in life as Christians is to see God, to explore the beauties of the eternal world that Jesus went to prepare for us. Before traveling to a foreign country we like to become acquainted with the places we plan to visit, the sights we hope to see. Since heaven will be our eternal dwelling place we should also be eager to learn about the things that will occupy our future home.

The Bible provides us with extensive information about heaven; all we have to do is research God's Word, the Holy Spirit will enlighten us with insight and understanding that are seldom heard from the pulpits today. Most preachers spend more time describing the horrors of hell, as important as that is for those who need to be warned of the awful consequences of not knowing Jesus and the hope of heaven.

Jesus encouraged His followers to set their affection on things above and not on the things of this earth," (Colossians 3:1-17).

Heaven is a place of jubilation, of celebration, rejoicing for victories won, an atmosphere of worship that honors God and glorifies Jesus Christ for our redemption. The awful agony of His suffering will be celebrated in glorious victory.

Heaven has always been a place of worship with the angels circling God's throne singing Holy, Holy, Holy, is the Lord!" Someone said the reason for this is that every time they circle God's Throne they see another view of God they had never seen before since God as Spirit is so vast, all we can add to this is to say, wow!

Wedding festivities have there own unique qualities of celebration, there is always great anticipation, even tears of joy, an awe struck audience beholding the bride as she makes her entrance to be presented to the bridegroom. As a lover of music I can hardly wait to participate in the enjoyment of all the heavenly sounds, as an artist I have always been intrigued with the many shades of color and light formation, in heaven there will be no need for the sun to shine to provide light, since Jesus is the light thereof.

As an entrepreneur, I look forward to behold the marriage supper of the Lamb, including the invited guests from every nation, kindred, tongue and people and the food that will be served, but most of all I want to celebrate the host who invited us to His banqueting table.

Most people will say they want to go to heaven when they die; there are also those who have told me otherwise in their ignorance. If these people would only understand what the consequences are to reject Jesus Christ and all that He has prepared for those who love Him they would indeed say otherwise, yet millions die without Christ every day.

To go to heaven, our flesh body has to die, if we are born again believers when we die our body will come forth at the first resurrection when the believers will be caught up in the clouds referred to as the rapture to be with the Lord forever in eternity. Our bodies will come forth from the grave a new and glorified body like that of Jesus when He was resurrected from the grave by His own power; it is that resurrection power that will unite us with Him in heaven.

Our Final Victory

Behold I show you a mystery; we shall not all sleep, but we shall be changed-in a moment, in the twinkling of an eye, at the last trumpet. For the trumpet will sound, and the dead will be raised incorruptible, and we shall be changed.

1 Corinthians 15:51-52).

One of the great questions in life has been, "what happens to us when we die?" Some people believe that death becomes the end of ones existence; still others believe that the body sleeps in the grave until the time of the resurrection. We need to know more than what some person thinks to know the truth, to know and understand truth we must believe the Word of God for ourselves, even Bible interpreters disagree on revealed truth and interpret the Bible according to their understanding. The Bible always speaks for itself and is not confusing if we read it for what it says, when we add our understanding and interpretation it will always result in confusion.

"To be absent from the body is to be present with the Lord,"

(2 Corinthians 5:7).

This is not confusing, it is clear, plain Bible truth. The moment of ones demise, the redeemed soul goes to be with Jesus in Paradise, the spirit of the unsaved go to hell.

To understand the mystery of Life and death, of heaven and hell we have to go to the Bible as our only source of truth. The Bible reveals exactly what happens after death, it explains in simple plain words what happens to those who have trusted Jesus Christ as their personal Savior and also reveals the fate of those who died as Christ rejecters.

To say we believe the Bible yet never read what the scripture reveals is to personally decide to remain ignorant. The Bible is clear in saying, *"choose you this day whom you will serve."* This becomes a daily decision to follow Jesus Christ with a faith and dependence for His redemptive work on the cross on our behalf. We either serve Jesus Christ by our belief about what He did for us and we say "yes" and agree to that by our confession of faith. People do not go to heaven because of their good works, there are people who might go to church faithfully all their lives yet miss heaven because they failed to acknowledge that Jesus is Lord of their life.

Hell has become a joke for many people, on the Day of Judgment this will not be a joke, it will be the saddest moment anyone has ever experienced, to become cut off from God and everything God is. Our death is as certain as the day of our birth and there is only one way to be prepared to die, that is to die in the Lord and every detail of our eternity will be well taken care of.

Religion Can Be Deceptive

Religion many times withholds truth. Religion without a personal relationship with Christ through the activity of the Holy Spirit is vain. The people I worked with in India were very religious but their religion was vain since it was not focused on Jesus Christ. I experienced the same thing in Trinidad, people who are devout and sincere but sincerely wrong. Billions of people have been lied to and deceived, and a great seduction has been taking place in our world today as never before. We will not go to heaven by the amount of money we give to an organization no matter how much good they do or how many souls they bring to Christ.

Jesus is the only way to salvation and heaven this is why He emphasized,

> *"I am the way, the truth, and the Life. No one comes to the Father but by me,"*

(John 14:6).

The god of this world has always blinded people with half truths. He uses scripture but distorts the scripture, he did this with Adam and Eve and he still uses these same tactics today even against the people of God who have come out of the world to deprive them of their rightful place in the Kingdom of God while here on earth and to do all he can to keep anyone from going to heaven.

The enemy blinds the world to the true gospel for his own personal reasons; he was cast out of heaven. He knows how beautiful and peaceful heaven is. The enemy of our soul does not want the light of God's revelation bringing individuals to acknowledge Jesus as Lord, he knows that God's coming Kingdom will banish him from his current position of world-wide influence, he knows he can never have what God offers to mankind, therefore his strategy is to keep as many people from going to heaven as he can.

God does not want anyone person to be ignorant about heaven, this is why the apostle Paul wrote,

> *"Brothers we do not want you to be ignorant about those who fell asleep or to grieve like the rest of men, who have no hope,"*

(1 Thessalonians 4:13).

There are as many ideas about death and where people go when they die as there are promises from the Bible to assure the believer of there promised eternal rest in heaven.

The reason that people don't understand God's Word is for the fact they don't know God. No one can explain the mysteries of God if they don't know Him in a personal relationship, even then there are mysteries withheld from the believer and only as the Holy Spirit opens the Word of God to anyone will we have greater insight to the mystery. This is why we can read the same passage for years and suddenly we see a whole new revelation of what God has been saying all along, the difference is, the Holy Spirit opened the Word into our spiritual understanding.

Only as we research what the Bible has to say about heaven will we understand in part the eternal dwelling place of the soul.

The Dying Thief Went to Paradise

It took less than thirty seconds for the dying thief to be transformed from being a criminal to a saint, all he did was to realize and acknowledge his worthiness of death for his crimes and that Jesus Christ was his only hope for redemption, all he did was to acknowledge his sin and confess Jesus as Lord, *"Lord remember me when you come into Your Kingdom"* Jesus' response was, *"Assuredly I say to you, today you will be with Me in Paradise,"* (Luke 23: 42-43).

Just where is Paradise? Song writers, professors of religion and many well meaning church leaders have done a great injustice to the theology of the Bible and the subject of heaven. For a born-again Christian to sing, "I'll meet you at the Great White Throne," is not where they want to be, this judgment is reserved for all Christ rejecters, the Christians will meet the Lord at "the judgment seat of Christ where they will be rewarded for their works and hear His Words,

"Well done good and faithful servant, enter into the joy of the Lord."

The judgment of ones faith takes place the moment we receive Jesus Christ as our Savior and there is no more condemnation when we appear before God; we will be judged for our works, the deeds we have done in the body.

Where is Paradise? The heavenly realm has many more dimensions than our finite minds can comprehend or imagine, Jesus Himself as the "Great I Am" is never subject to time or space, He is eternal, He is not limited to anything, He is God, and this is why we need to allow Him to be just that, our responsibility is not to try to figure out the facts of God, God is! He always will be God, and *"He rewards those who diligently seek Him."*

Jesus said something very significant about Paradise in referring to the Father's house when He said,

> *"Let not your heart be troubled; you believe God believe also in Me. In My Father house are many mansions; if it were not so, I would have told you, I go to prepare a place for you. And if I go to prepare a place for you, I will come again to receive you unto Myself; that where I am, there you may be also,"* (John 14:1-3).

What Are the City's Dimensions?

The size of the City of Gold, the New Jerusalem that the angel gave to John was equal to 1500 miles long, wide and high.

> *"And he that talked with me had a gold reed to measure the city, its gates and its walls. The city is laid out as a square; its length is as great as its breadth, and the height are equal. Then he measured its wall:*

one hundred and forty-four cubits, according to the measure of a man, that is, of an angel. The construction of its wall was of jasper; and the city was pure gold, like clear glass. The foundations of the wall of the city were adorned with all kinds of precious stones; the first foundation was jasper, the second sapphire, the third chalcedony, the fourth emerald, the fifth sardonyx, the sixth sardius, the seventh chrysolite, the eight beryl, the ninth topaz, the tenth chrysoprase, the eleventh jacinth, and the twelfth amethyst. The twelve gates were twelve pearls; each individual gate was of one pearl, and the street of the city was pure gold, like transparent glass,"

(Revelation 21:15-21).

To better understand the extent of the New Jerusalem and its size compare this as a metropolis stretching from Canada to Mexico and from the Appalachians Mountains to California.

What is the Significance of the City's Gates?

The City has "a great high wall with twelve gates and with twelve angels at each gate, on the gates are written the names of the twelve tribes of Israel.

John describes a natural wonder in the center of the New Jerusalem:

"The river of the water of life, as clear as crystal, flowing from the throne of God and of the Lamb down the middle of the great city is the center of life, the source of this powerful stream is the throne of God, occupied by the Lamb, Jesus Christ.

*On each side of the river stood the tree of life,
bearing twelve crops of fruit, yielding fruit every
month and the leaves were for the healing of the
nations,"*

(Revelation 22:2).

In the Garden of Eden the tree appears to have been a
source of ongoing life, Adam and Eve were created by God
to live forever. Once they sinned, they were banned from
the garden and the presence of the tree of life to experience
spiritual death, since that day death has reigned throughout
history and mankind was without hope until Jesus Christ
came into the world and provided for *"whosoever will,"*
eternal life.

Heaven has been the hope of God's people for ages past,
hope for a better life, for peace and rest, but most of all our
hope is to be in the presence of Jesus Christ and all that eternity provides for us.

We do not want to make heaven more or less than what
God has made it since it is beyond our human comprehen-
sion, the least we can do is to be prepared for the time when
the death angel will call us out of this life. If we die in the
Lord, we will also dwell with Him in His City of Gold that
He has prepared for those who love Him.

*"Eye has not seen, nor ear heard, nor have entered
into the heart of man the things which God has
prepared for those who love Him,"*

(1 Corinthians 2: 9).

A Prepared City, For a Prepared People

Before we can enter the City of God, we are instructed in detail about the need to be prepared, from the day that I can remember my heart was set toward heaven, but I do not want to become so heavenly minded that I'm no good to the Lord here on the earth. It is easy to fantasize about heaven; this is all a part of our inspirational meditation.

Jesus told many stories about heaven and our after-life, His entire life was spent to make possible our eternity with Him and He had much to say about the importance of being prepared, how to invest treasure in His Kingdom.

In the Bible we are instructed how to live and how to prepare for our demise when we give an account of how we have lived and served Him. Many Christians have missed God's best for their lives through their disobedience, but God always has mercy.

The City of God is made of pure gold which symbolizes the holiness and sacredness of God, everything in heaven will be pure and holy and every Christian looks forward to seeing the beauty of heaven, but the most grandest moment of all will be to behold the unveiling and the revealing of God Himself as He is, to see Jesus face to face including His nail scarred hands, to behold the Holy Spirit who kept us from falling and who restored us when we fell while we lived our lives on the earth, to see the heavenly hosts, the Old Testament saints and our loved ones who had passed from this life so long ago.

The entire Genesis through Revelation story of God and man will come into focus, the redeemed joining in worship, praise and adoration for the great victories won by the power of the blood of the Lamb who is now the light and glory of heaven itself.

Can you imagine what it will be like to observe Abraham as the father of many nations meeting his descendants? An entourage of millions of redeemed from his time in history who also became faithful followers of Christ and to celebrate in that victory.

Surly as the author of the many Psalms that have inspired our faith and prayer life will also inspire us as we see Him giving thanks to the Lord for the great victories won in the many battles he fought in the natural realm as well as the spiritual victories he won as a result of the Lord hearing his pray of confession as recorded in Psalm 51.

The jubilation and the glory of worship, the privilege of serving in whatever capacity that may be, to be involved in the activity of heaven is simply beyond our capacity to imagine, but this is the glorious hope that lies within our spirit to some day after this life is over to explore the beauty of eternity. Please don't live your life careless, haphazard and Godless that you will miss it, surrender your life to Jesus Christ! Allow the Holy Spirit to prepare your soul to meet the Lord.

Prayer for Salvation

Pray this Prayer with Me

Heavenly Father I come to you in Jesus' name, I confess my great need for your redeeming love, your forgiving grace, set me free from the things that have distracted me from Your presence, if there is anything in my life that is not pleasing to You, reveal this to me, I confess any sin that I may have committed known or unknown I want to be completely cleansed by the power of Your blood. Help me to focus on things eternal, teach me what it really means to *"set my affection on things above, and not on the things of this earth."*

My heart is overwhelmed when I think of who You are and all You do for me, when I come into Your presence. I always feel your Holy Spirit speaking into my spirit, but I become so easily distracted by things around me, sometimes I become discouraged but I never want to give up, I would really desire to have a deeper relationship with You now that I'm growing older.

I sincerely trust you with my soul and the things about life and death that I can't understand or comprehend, yet I believe. Teach me Your Word and give me an understanding heart to know You better.

When I pray receive my prayer words and may they always ascend to Your Throne as a sweet smelling fragrance to be acceptable to You. I will praise and worship You for who You are, I commit and surrender my life to You and ask You to lead me according to Your will.

Thank you for hearing my requests, safeguard my life by Your Holy Spirit, keep me in Your perfect will and please give Your holy angels charge over me. I love you Lord! Thanks for hearing my prayer in Jesus' name, amen.

Your Personal Invitation

If you have never accepted Jesus Christ as your personal Savior I invite you to receive Him right now, just say, "Lord Jesus I am a sinner, I'm not sure that I am a born again Christian, sometimes I feel so lost and I don't want to die without knowing you, please come into my heart and save my soul, I believe that you went to the cross and died for my sin, that you were raised from the dead and ascended to heaven to prepare a place for me, I surrender my life to you now. Thank you for saving my soul and help me to live a victorious Christian life, in Jesus' name. Amen.

Lord I sign my name on this line to believe that you signed my name in Your Book of Life!

Signed_____

Believe what the Bible has to say about your confession of faith in Christ, repent from your sins follow the Lord in Christian baptism and become involved in a soul-winning church fellowship.

"That if you confess with your mouth the Lord Jesus Christ and believe in your heart that God has raised Him from the dead, you will be saved. For with the heart man believes unto righteousness, and with the mouth confession is made unto salvation,"

(Romans 10:9-10).

End Notes

All scripture references are taken from the Christian Life Bible, New King James version.

Thomas Nelson Publishers.

Please Note

I do not capitalize the name satan since I refuse to give him honorable mention. My only reference sources include excerpts from the Christian Life Bible foot notes.

Chapter's thirteen and fourteen include excerpts from the New Illustrated Bible Dictionary.

Thomas Nelson Publisher

Only as the Holy Spirit recalled to memory from the archives of my mind along with the common knowledge I retained from my years of ministry experiences, including the wisdom and spiritual teaching of others through the years was I able to bring this inspiration to the printed page.

Reproductions for **The King of Kings** oil painting are available in various sizes. For information on size and prices contact-

David Huyard
541 New York Avenue
Harrisonburg, Virginia 22801

Telephone 540-433-9481
Email address <u>davidhuyard@aol.com</u>

1 Reproductions of this oil painting are available
in full color and in any size from the artist.
Contact davidhuyard@aol.com

3 Thirty years after my vision I was able to take a photo
of what the Lord showed me while preaching on the
island of Antigua, in the West Indies.

Mom @ Dad Huyard
Photo taken by Lord Snowden which appeared
2   in McCalls Magazine, April 1972

4 David @ Anna Mary Huyard in their recording studio

Breinigsville, PA USA
15 October 2009
225926BV00001B/1/P